DESERT ENGLAND

DESERT ENGLAND

DAVID WILLIAMS

APEX PUBLISHING LTD

First published in 2008 by
Apex Publishing Ltd
PO Box 7086, Clacton on Sea, Essex, CO15 5WN, United Kingdom

www.apexpublishing.co.uk

British Library Cataloguing-in-Publication Data
A catalogue record for this book
is available from the British Library

ISBN 1-906358-08-7   978-1-906358-08-2

Typeset in 10pt Times New Roman

Production Manager: Chris Cowlin

Cover Design: Siobhan Smith

Printed and bound in Great Britain

To Emlyn Williams
I miss you dad.

FOREWORD

A few years back I had a chance meeting with David Williams during which he asked me how I personally went about writing the books I have written. The answer was simple; we all have at least one good story to tell but it is having the dedication to sit down and put pen to paper or thump your fingertips upon a keyboard in order to tell it, that is the hard bit. That dedication comes from having a belief in your work, a belief that the story is worth telling and that others will enjoy reading it.

Over the past decade some of the world's foremost publishers finally had their eyes opened to the fact that a whole new market, a whole movement if you like were not being catered for. Nowadays the boom in books relating to football fans and in particular football hooliganism culture, both factual and fiction, has grown to such an extent that all the leading bookshops have dedicated shelving space allocated to that movement; something that when looking back would have been unthinkable in the late eighties to mid-nineties when the game's supporters were seen by society as being the scum of the earth. Oh how times and football have changed!

Thankfully David Williams had the dedication and belief to sit down and write his story and so his book Desert England is now added to those shelves. Mills and Boon it most definitely is not. I hope you enjoy it, I certainly did and I feel privileged to have been one of the first to have read it.

Keep the faith.

Eddy Brimson

Prelude

It could not have been a more perfect autumn day to be outdoors. The sun, although not at its most powerful, was doing its best to delay the onset of the snow season and many were taking advantage of the extended summer to browse through the high street shops of the pedestrian precinct.

"Mama, mama," came the bullish request for attention from a small girl as she tugged her young mother's dress towards the toys staring from out of the shop window and onto the main street.

The mother, more interested in eying up the latest winter fashions, reluctantly surrendered and followed her infant towards the magnetic draw of colourful bears and dolls that filled the shop window.

It was idyllic. Elderly couples linked arms as they leisurely wandered down the paved road, merely filling in some spare midweek hours. Young mothers were everywhere, making the most of the final throws of warm weather with their young children while the men were away at work. School kids - who probably should have been at school - were hanging around anywhere a bench could be found, while tourists mingled with the locals but, like in any city in the world, they still looked like tourists and stuck out amidst the crowd.

But something on the wind sent a shiver down the young mother's spine and she reacted by rubbing the back of her neck and looking uneasily over her shoulder at the busy street. While her daughter's attention was firmly fixed on the shop window, she sensed something was not right.

In the distance - no, not that far away - she could hear what sounded like a hundred raised voices. Other bystanders looked at one another in bewilderment as the rumble grew louder. The bell on the nearby cathedral struck out the first of 12 chimes to signal midday had arrived, but it was barely noticed as the mother became increasingly uncomfortable and took a step closer to within touching distance of her daughter.

The shouts intensified. They seemed to have increased in number and were definitely getting nearer. People around her were concerned and turned their collective gaze to the top of the street. Nothing could be seen, which only heightened the tension further.

The mother grabbed her young child's arm, more to comfort herself than her offspring who was still more interested in the toys rather than the mysterious roars cascading from out of view and down the street.

Some people seemed frozen to the spot, staring up the street, inquisitively waiting. Others feared the worst and started to move in unison in one direction, looking over their shoulders in fear as they shuffled along.

The bell struck two, then three and in a split second the young mother's life was about to change forever.

A huge smash, which sounded like a large windowpane being obliterated into a thousand pieces, was heard and the noises descended on the street as a terrifying sight burst into view. All around her, shuffling walks turned into sprints for freedom as young and old fled a tidal wave of horror that filled the street from one side to the next. Only it wasn't water that was about to engulf them, but hundreds of rampaging men with fists and feet flaying in all directions and at anything that stood in their way. The terrified mother picked up her child with all her strength and headed in the opposite direction. The child was hysterical, her mother screaming as the tsunami crushed everything in its path. She dared not look over her shoulder. She saw what had happened to the other stragglers who were now getting battered where they fell, no matter what their age or sex.

But the weight of her offspring was slowing her down as she struggled to keep up with the fleeing hordes. Before she had the chance to duck into a shop, she felt a blow to the back of her head and fell to the floor, still grasping her terrified child whom she shielded as first one, then two kicks connected to the back of her ribcage. She held on to her child for dear life, screaming with terror as she saw hundreds of pairs of legs run past her.

She closed her eyes and pulled her child tightly to her body as all around her windows were smashed and innocent people were thrown to the ground and beaten. Hundreds of, or maybe a thousand, grown men rampaged in one direction and demolished anything in their track. Who and what could have started such a ferocious rage?

Then, as quickly as it had appeared, the tidal wave of terror disappeared out of view. Breathless and bruised, the mother rolled onto her back with her child still cradled in her arms, thankfully unhurt apart from a few scratches on her hands and knees from the initial tumble to the ground in her mother's arms. The mother gasped for breath. Her ribs were damaged, several probably broken. Blood seeped onto the paved road. It leaked from the wound opened up by the initial blow to the head. It would need stitches for sure.

The street lay silent, stunned as the wounded gingerly got to their feet. The mother remained motionless, still reluctant to let go of her precious child. The bells struck 11, and finally 12. A war had just swept through this sleepy Alpine city. Like any war, it didn't distinguish between men, women or children; the young or the old. Anyone in its way paid the penalty and many had.

And there were still eight hours left 'til kick off.

Chapter 1

There is something about a high-profile football match that has John Milton on edge. Detective Inspector John Milton, that is. Head of the English anti-soccer hooliganism task force and the man who, more than any other man on the face of the planet on this particular day, probably wished that he had steered well clear of the 'sensible' career path he was treading.

"Position camera two onto that group there," he said with a twinge of agitation in his strong southern voice. Pointing to the screen over the shoulder of a uniformed officer, Milton watched as the shaven heads and weathered faces of a small group of England fans became clearer as the CCTV camera focused in.

"What are they doing there?" pondered Milton while slipping a finger under his pale blue tie to loosen a noose that had pulled ever tighter as the sultry September day dragged on.

Peeling away to no one in particular, he barked his orders: "Okay. Get some boys over there and chuck them back in the away end … and for Christ's sake get some air con into this room."

For two hours, Milton and his team of eagle-eyed officers had stared at a wall of TV screens covering just about every member of the 40,000 crowd in the stadium outside. Despite it being Switzerland in the middle of September, the temporary construction lofted high above the halfway line was heating up, but that could have been attributed just as much to the tension inside than to the muggy autumn evening on the exterior.

The calm, almost laid-back atmosphere in the stadium was of stark contrast to the mayhem that had unfolded in the hours building up to the game, and it fanned the flames burning inside Milton, who was feeling the pressure of 12 months of limited results … well, if the truth be known, no results.

A bead of sweat rolled down the side of his face, traversing the lines and wrinkles that had become ever more visible over the past year. It stalled for a moment on the bottom of his chin and gathered weight before dropping onto his hand as he leaned over a flimsy table in the middle of the room. Not even beads of sweat could break his stare at the wall of screens, which were busily zooming in and out of every nook and cranny of the stadium.

"Where are they?" he mumbled under his breath while interspersing glares at the screen with glances through the huge window looking out over the pitch. "Where, where, where, where, WHERE are they?" his voice growing in volume before his fist landed on the table, which in turn buckled to the floor, taking with it a tray of drinks and sandwiches politely laid on by the hosting Swiss police.

For a moment his fellow officers turned their inquisitive heads, but on seeing the frustration that Milton was visibly exuding they returned to their work like frightened schoolboys.

Half turning to the door, Milton realised that it was probably the biggest act of violence demonstrated within the stadium all evening, and running his hand through his ever receding hairline he conceded that he had been beaten once again.

"Bastards," he mumbled under his breath, but just loud enough for the seven officers from both his own task force and the local constabulary present to hear. They buried themselves back into their surveillance work for fear of incurring the wrath of their commanding officer.

Milton knew he was going to get it with both barrels when he flew back to HQ in London the following day. The jobs didn't come much bigger than this. This was the Olympic Gold of all police jobs.

With less than five months before FIFA, the world governing body for football, announced its decision as to which country would host the 2006 World Cup, it was neck-and-neck between old enemies Germany and England. England had all the ingredients for a successful bid: the stadiums, erected at a cost of hundreds of millions of pounds to the taxpayer, the hotels, the entertainment and, of course, the history and tradition. There was just one thing that had become a thorn in the side of the bid and it was a thorn of javelin proportions.

Since launching its bid two years earlier, English hooligans had wreaked havoc on every away game that the national team had been a part of, and Milton was the man assigned to intervene. A policeman with an impeccable track record and 12 years of distinguished service under his belt, and commended and promoted for his undercover work in thwarting a major drugs operation, Milton was tailor-made for the job. His late father was a police chief, and his father before that, but the one he had tried to impress the most was the father of his wife, a recently retired Deputy Assistant

Commissioner of the Metropolitan Police Force who judged Milton's achievements against those of his own.

This assignment was to be his big breakthrough. The hooliganism trail had become the biggest ongoing news story since the Gulf War and surely the man who brought an end to it all would be treated as a war hero ... and rewarded so too? That sort of potential praise was exactly what attracted Milton to the assignment in the first place but it had started to wear thin. He would be lucky if he got away with holding a lollipop stick and helping school kids cross the road for the rest of his career given his progress over the past year.

Four away matches, four incidents of mass hooliganism, hundreds of arrests and thousands of banning orders restricting known troublemakers from travelling abroad, and yet the Switzerland v. England match presented the worst incidents yet. Milton knew the stakes had been raised. No longer was it a bunch of lager louts on a jolly. It had become more organised than that, but who and where the organisers were had become the focal point of Milton's life. Twelve months and millions of pounds later, he was no nearer to a solution than the armchair know-it-alls who universally proclaimed "idiots" and "lock 'em up" after watching the events unfold on the 6 o'clock news.

Milton knew, as he looked out of the surveillance room window, that those organisers were out there somewhere, probably laughing at the inability of Britain's biggest and most expensive international police operation to thwart them; smirking because they had got away with it - again.

The pressure had got to everyone and one young sergeant, Peter Miller, was almost ready to throw in the towel. He whispered to his right, "It's like looking for a piece of hay in a bloody haystack," which was met by a rush of air pushed from the nostrils of his comrade - a kind of muffled smirk-cum-sigh.

Sitting in a corner of the Portakabin, which resembled a high-tech scout hut, Milton rested his chin on his hands and reflected on the day's bizarre events: seventeen police officers hospitalised; 53 innocent bystanders injured; over 100 beer-swilling Englishmen arrested; and damage to the beautiful city of Zurich running into hundreds of thousands of pounds. But the damage to the British economy would run into billions should England miss out on clinching the World Cup 2006, and FIFA had warned the English authorities that its patience was running out. The tired old 'minority' excuse had become hard for the footballing powers-that-be to swallow. Downtown

Zurich resembled a city that had just welcomed a battalion from the Anarchist Revolutionary Guard. A minority? Not anymore; this was more like an army.

Windows smashed, shops turned upside down and innocent men, women and children beaten as an outpouring of indiscriminate rage swept through an otherwise tranquil city. These people's lives would never be the same again and Milton believed that the perpetrators should be charged with war crimes, never mind the slap on the wrist and the free trip home that probably lay in wait for them.

There was an eerie silence in the surveillance room as each and every member present felt the pressure that their superior was under. Still glued to the screens, the officers were determined to bring some sort of relief to their respected boss who had stood by each and every one of them during a difficult period.

Suddenly the silence was sliced open by Sergeant Thomas Waite, eager to be the bearer of good news for his embattled guv'nor. The 28-year-old had probably grown closer to the boss over the past year than any of his colleagues.

"Sir, there's the fella we filmed chucking the police helmet through the newsagent's window this afternoon," he said, focusing his screen on a tough-looking, beer-bellied lout in his late thirties. The man, sticking a customary English soccer solute of two fingers up at the opposing fans, was seemingly uninterested in the action on the pitch, his head and body aimed towards the Swiss fans located on the other side of the dividing security fence.

Milton shook his head as he rose to his feet to inspect the discovery. "Who do these idiots think they are? They have a wife and kids at home; probably a desk job too; but as soon as they get the stamp of a new country in their passports they become animals, the lowest sort of scum. Call themselves patriotic? Their grandfathers would turn in their graves if they could see how the loved ones they had fought for had turned out. It makes me sick." Then, with a deep breath, almost a sigh of despondency, Milton decided: "Haul him in, Waite. He can join the rest of the boys for bed and breakfast."

As he slowly returned to his corner of solace, Milton heard Waite dish out the instructions in slow, easy-to-understand English to his Swiss counterpart on the other end of the radio. "That is row X, seat 42, in the Alpine Stand." A cackled reply was met by, "No! Row X, not Rolex. Do not go to the Rolex Stand. It is the Alpine Stand! Row X, seat 42, in the Alpine Stand."

The cackled reply seemingly understood the instructions on this occasion, but Milton could not help but smirk to himself and thought that, as soon as the transmission had finished, the overworked Swiss sergeant on the other end of the walkie-talkie would turn to his colleagues and remark, "Fucking English!" A common sentiment Europe-wide when it came to football.

Nevertheless, within seconds the surveillance room watched on the screen as a heavy-handed mob of police waded into the crowd, grabbed the identified offender and herded him away, much to the annoyance of the man's comrades who kicked, punched and spat on the well-padded officers. Not surprisingly, their reply with a few swipes of their rubber sticks brought the short burst of trouble to an end.

Milton watched and almost enjoyed the show in a bizarre and sadistic sort of way. For a moment he imagined he was watching real-life TV in the comfort of his own South London home, with a mug of tea handed to him by his loving wife as he stroked the tummy of his Labrador, and his two boys looking on from their toys strewn out over the large sheepskin rug.

Fat chance. His daydream was pinched by the thought that millions, if not billions, of people across the world also would have witnessed this spectacle on television, and would observe dozens more like it over the coming days.

That thought brought a touch of embarrassment to Milton. It was a thought that men the same age as him, and some even older, could bring such disgrace to a country they claimed to love and represent. Did they not realise what harm they were causing their beloved England?

As his superiors had drilled into him after the previous four humiliations abroad since he had taken over, the World Cup 2006 would create thousands of jobs, bring in billions of tourism pounds and one simply could not put a price on the hundreds of hours of worldwide television exposure. It would underline England as one of the world's great countries and tourist destinations, not to mention Europe's most desirable country to live in.

Madness!

Milton knew he had failed miserably so far, but with only two more away matches remaining until FIFA's D-Day he also knew that for now his position was probably safe. It was too late to appoint a new task force and the powers that be had decided it was shit or bust with Milton's operation.

If his results didn't improve, what would happen after the next two games was simply not worth contemplating right now, but 'humiliation' and 'back on the beat' echoed in Milton's mind far too often for his own liking these days. If he could escape from it all, he would. But he knew he could not.

Milton's long stare at the floor was broken by a sharp blast from the referee's final whistle from the pitch outside. He was up and out of the door before the first set of players had shaken hands on the pitch.

"Make sure we've got all the surveillance stuff from the ground and the shopping centres ready for taking back with us tomorrow," was all he could muster, not wanting to catch the overworked eyes of his colleagues as he clumsily grabbed a bundle of papers and set a course for the exit, followed by Waite.

As he left the stadium for the temporary lock-up set up by the local establishment to house the expected English troublemakers, he could not help but think that the referee's whistle had not only signified a defeat for the English team on the field but also a defeat for the English police force off it. The latter defeat, though, was possibly more damaging to the nation than the football team's could ever be.

* * *

Walking into the old school building, which had been renovated at great cost to accommodate its unwilling English visitors, Milton felt a relief to be away from the ground. With Waite at his side like a loyal sheepdog, the pair bounced time-old theories off each other in the hope of finding the answer, which seemed to be further away now than when they were first assigned to this mess in what seemed like a lifetime ago.

"Sir, they were just a bunch of thugs looking for a ruck," deduced Waite. "How can anyone stop a few thousand grown men going on the rampage?"

"Come on, Waite. You know better than that. That was cold, calculated destruction. It was organised. It was callous and it was successful," replied Milton, as he approached the wall-sized reinforced windows housing the arrested English hooligans in the former school's gymnasium.

They knew its layout well having visited the facility several times during the week building up to the match. As with any England game, trouble was expected and the local police cells would not have been able to cope.

Assessing the assembled hooligans, Milton concluded that they looked a sad and pathetic bunch of individuals, caged in like the animals they were and spitting and staring at any passer-by that looked in.

"These men couldn't have orchestrated the destruction we saw this afternoon. Most of these men are cowards, taking out the frustrations of their inadequacies at home on some innocent foreign land under the banner of football."

Looking back at the gathering of bloodied, pot-bellied, tattooed men hanging around like school kids in detention, Milton was under no illusion that the big fish had got away once again.

"These aren't the men we are looking for. These are simply soldiers, and soldiers are ineffective unless they have generals calling the shots. These men couldn't organise a gang bang in a brothel on pay day."

The pair continued to walk through the bland corridors and into an office, which was formerly the headmaster's room. Through the orange door sat Commissioner Oleg Von Wolf. Peering at Milton and Waite over a walrus moustache and rose red cheeks, the Swiss Police Chief took his knee-length leather boots off the heavy oak desk and shuffled upright on the arrival of his visitors, who by now resembled a downtrodden Oliver Twist creeping towards his domineering master for a hiding that's inevitable.

"May I congratulate you and your English thugs," said Von Wolf.

Milton had seen enough Second World War movies to realise that the Commissioner's tongue was firmly rooted into his cheek.

"Your hooligans have succeeded in destroying one of Central Europe's most beautiful cities and all we have to show is this bunch of overweight, drunken idiots who look like they have just got off an Airtours flight from SPAIN!"

Von Wolf's speech gathered momentum as his voice grew louder and Milton knew this was nothing compared with the roasting he would receive at the hands of his own superiors within the next 24 hours.

"With all due respect, sir, we have worked on this operation together for the past six weeks, so now is not the time to be deflecting blame from yourself," Milton replied in defiance.

The retort was practical, but he may just as well have had a bowl in his hand asking for more broth for all the good it served.

"So, Detective Inspector, you are blaming us for this destruction? You think it was our people who smashed up everything they could get their hands on? Was it our people who drank the pubs dry all afternoon? Was it our people who punched and kicked innocent women and children who were going about their daily business? I think not, Detective Inspector. You do not have a problem on your hands, you have a disease, and unless you find some sort of cure soon it will become an epidemic among your countrymen.

"We installed over 200,000 francs worth of CCTV cameras and manoeuvred over 1,200 full-time officers and reservists into the city at a cost of God knows what. This was the biggest police operation we have ever staged and it failed, Detective Inspector. I am at a loss to ask what more we could have done?"

But Milton, looking at the floor and shuffling his feet like a chastised altar boy, was taken aback by what was next said by the militarist Von Wolf.

"That said though, I do feel sorry for you, Detective Inspector. I have a press conference in 30 minutes and there is nothing to be gained from criticising each other. Worry not, Detective Inspector, you will come out of this smelling of roses ... red roses I suppose you would prefer as an Englishman? You are not to blame for the actions of others. Damage limitation is the order of the day, or we will end up looking as stupid as each other."

"Thank you, sir," Milton replied to the first bit of decent news he had received in days. "I would like to speak to some of the prisoners now, sir."

Pointing to a burly uniformed officer positioned by the door, Von Wolf added in his best exaggerated Queen's English, "Oh, Detective Inspector." Milton and Waite paused. "Good luck, old boy. I think you will need it."

The three men walked back down the corridor towards the gymnasium where the England fans were detained.

At the entrance, which looked like it had been kicked more times than a Brazilian centre forward, stood two armed officers who nodded at the group of men and guided them with an outstretched arm to a classroom opposite. Inside, the lout, arrested earlier in the evening after being caught in the ground by the surveillance camera, sat with his head bowed down and two officers shouting at him from the other side of the desk.

The thug looked as though he had been dragged through a hedge backwards, and then forwards again just for good measure. Small cuts bled on his closely shaved, balding head, a signal that he had not given in lightly to his arrest, and he was almost relieved to see two 'fellow' Englishmen enter, albeit two coppers.

"Thank you, officers," Milton gestured to the two Swiss interrogators, who in turn put on their caps and walked towards the exit. On the way out, one turned and spat in the direction of the shamed man and grunted, "I hope the Germans get the World Cup."

At that precise moment that comment could have been supported by just about every footballing nation in Europe, in fact in the world. Earlier in the day such a remark would have seen the man reply with a barrage of punches, but he now seemed to accept that he was beaten.

"What's your name?" enquired Waite after flipping a chair back to front and straddling the backrest.

Somewhat ashamedly, the man raised his head to reveal a puffed-up, blackening eye that was welling up with water.

"John Simons," he replied with a whisper, barely loud enough to hear.

"What's your story, John Simons? Over here for a ruck or to watch football? The evidence we have could put you away for a very long time, sunshine."

Simons sat silent, suspecting a red herring had just been thrown at him, but he was soon forced into talking.

"Got something against newsagents eh, John Simons?" added Waite. The penny dropped, as the perpetrator realised his earlier act of vandalism had been caught ... and so had he.

"Okay, okay," Simons piped up. "What do you want to know?"

Milton, who had been pacing around the room like an inquisitive parent, suddenly realised that he had someone who was ready to squeal like a baby.

"We want to know exactly what you've been up to today," he said, darting from the back of the classroom.

"Tell us a story, John Simons, about your little trip to Switzerland and we will see if we can get you out of here tonight," Milton said in a sarcastic parental voice.

It did the trick. Simons went on to share that he had flown into Zurich the day before with a group of fellow Chelsea fans. He had taken two days off work from his job in the city and was expecting to catch the midnight flight back to Heathrow. Needless to say, he could forget about work for the week, or in fact for the rest of the year.

After a heavy night of bars and strip clubs, Simons and his merry men had retired back to their bed and breakfast in readiness for a hard day of drinking before the match. They had started with a beer to wash down their 9.00 a.m. continental breakfast and had continued drinking at the hotel before heading into the town centre. There they had joined around 8,000 other Englishmen who had flown, driven or caught the train in to watch this European Cup qualifier.

"Rumour was going around that trouble was going to kick off but none of us was interested in joining in," he said. "That's the truth. But before you knew it, at around noon, pandemonium broke out with fists, bottles, kicks, you name it, flying everywhere. We didn't know who was who and we just got caught up in the melee. I lost it. I really lost it. Maybe it was the beer, maybe the adrenalin, but I shouldn't have got involved. I just shouldn't have done it ..."

"Boohoo, pal," interrupted Waite. "Who started the trouble? Give us names, places, inside leg sizes and you may be able to see your kids open their Christmas presents."

Simons suddenly swallowed the magnitude of his dire situation and realised that his earlier actions were enough for him to suffer a lengthy stay in a Swiss jail.

He sighed, "I don't know. That's the truth. All the lads from the football clubs that used to be the ringleaders are banned from travelling now. Have been for a long time. Rumour has it that there's this group of men. Trained men who love nothing more than this sort of thing. These men come in, cause a ruck and disappear without trace. Nobody knows who they are, where they come from or what club they support. People that have seen these lads in action reckon they're mustard. They fight like you've never seen fighting before and the rest of us just get caught up in the excitement; it snowballs from there."

The words sank into Milton's head without a single word of reply. It pointed to a theory that had burned in his throat like CS gas since he had got involved in this whole mess. He knew that football violence was orchestrated, organised, but could it be that there was some group, some force of trained men pulling the strings? Surely not. He shook his head towards the direction of Simons, grabbed Waite by the arm and headed for the door.

"This is getting worse, Waite. We are in for big shit tomorrow at HQ!"

* * *

Back in his hotel room, Simons' comments still haunted him. They repeated in his mind over and over again. Even under the cold bursts of shower water, Milton could not remove any of the day's events from his mind and he knew he was in for a restless night before catching his 8.00 a.m. plane back to London to face the music.

Slipping on a white bathrobe without towelling off, Milton crashed onto the bed and grabbed the remote control to watch the inevitable. It was now well after midnight. His hair was still dripping onto his shoulders and bed, which was covered by an off-white coloured duvet.

CNN, BBC, SKY, not to mention the dodgy European channels, preached the same reaction stories about the 'English disease'; FIFA's patience running out; and responses from the bespectacled German politicians stating that England should be removed from the running to host the 2006 World Cup and the tournament handed to them.

He decided to remain with CNN. Surely the Yanks have no sustained interest in this? he thought wrongly to himself.

The pretty lady reporter was finishing off her summing up of the day's events while standing outside the stadium: "No serious incidents have been reported since before the game and there is an uneasy calm over Zurich tonight where the residents are asking 'why?' and finding it hard to believe that this is all over a game of football after all." She paused, stared at the camera, and then wrapped up: "This is …"

The name faded out as Milton's head crashed against the pillow. Although tired, his eyes were wide open, as though he had taken a wrap of speed washed down with a pint of Red Bull. As he stared at the ceiling, he was suddenly propped upright again by the anchorman's announcement that Swiss Police Chief Commissioner, Oleg Von Wolf, was about to make a live announcement.

Looking his pompous best with the world's media at his mercy, Von Wolf declared: "We believe that our operation was a success. Over 100 English supporters were arrested and we will be handing their names over to our English friends in the anti-hooliganism task force. We are disappointed by the levels of violence that we have witnessed this afternoon but would like to say that our Swiss men and women who were on active duty have performed admirably and I would like to offer my congratulations for a job well done. I wish those in hospital my best wishes and will be visiting them personally later tonight. That is all I have to say on this matter for now."

As hordes of tape recorders and microphones rushed towards the burly chief, he hastily left his podium and scurried behind the two large wooden doors of the police headquarters.

Milton knew he had just heard utter bullshit, but the Commissioner, as promised, had kept to his word by not criticising Milton's operation. The two had become professional friends after all. Von Wolf felt sorry for his more junior counterpart. For that he was grateful as he towelled his dripping locks.

However, Milton also knew that Von Wolf had a hidden agenda. During their six-week build-up to the game, Von Wolf had confided to Milton that he had less than eight months left to serve in office, and he intended to spend his retirement in politics. It was hardly surprising, then, that he was heading to the hospital to see his wounded officers at 1.00 a.m. followed by a hungry pack of local media. He would probably look for a baby or two to kiss along the way.

Milton's eyelids became heavier as he again fell back into the sanctuary of his king-size bed. All he could think of again before reaching the escapism of sleep was: "I am in for big shit tomorrow!"

At that point, he had never felt so alone in his life.

Chapter 2

The flight home was made in solace. Although flanked by colleagues, apart from the brief hellos at the airport very little was said on the plane for the two-hour journey back. Most of Milton's team had travelled direct to the airport from the surveillance offices and the temporary lock-up where they had assisted in the interrogations.

Milton's night's sleep had been interrupted more times than he would like to admit and he had not required the hotel's wake-up call at 5.00 a.m. either, his restless mind ensuring he was wide awake long before the sun came up.

His concerns for the assignment had turned into concerns about his job. He had somehow managed to convince himself on the journey home that this would be his last day on the force and he would be dismissed. He turned his thoughts to his wife, who was putting constant pressure on him to advance through the ranks. She had her own selfish agenda though. Maggie's daily routine after dropping the kids off at school included a coffee with her friends, whose favourite topic of conversation was the size of their husband's pay cheques. Keeping up with the Joneses had proved to be just as difficult in his private life as the assignment had become in his professional life. Milton no longer had a corner in which to hide and he was beginning to think that something had to give soon. His wife was simply not the same exciting young woman she used to be.

He then thought about his father-in-law and how much he had started to resent the man whom he had once spent so much time trying to impress.

"By the time I was your age, John, I was being groomed for the Commissioner's post," was the last thing he had said when the in-laws paid their weekly visit for dinner before his departure to Switzerland. "You really need to be more ambitious in your work, John."

His comments were supported by agreeing nods from his wife and mother-in-law, who in turn looked to Milton for a reaction.

"Of course, sir. The Met is my life too and I want to be successful," he had replied, lying through his back teeth.

A year earlier he was indeed ambitious and would have uttered that same statement with complete sincerity. Now, however, his outlook was very different. Discovering the ringleaders behind the soccer hooliganism had become his life and a lot more of a personal mission. It was starting to put a strain on his creaking marriage and he would quite happily spend the rest of his working days cleaning London Underground toilets so long as it meant cracking this case first.

The taxi journey from Heathrow to Scotland Yard was not long enough for Milton to get his mind around a plausible excuse that would save his career. And the walk to his boss's office went with a blink. It was time to face the music.

"Come in, Detective Inspector," said Deputy Assistant Commissioner Steven Dobson, the man Milton had to answer to in a chain of command that finished at the very top with the Prime Minister.

The problem with Deputy Assistant Commissioner Dobson was that God had presented him with a very unfortunate lisp. He had undergone speech therapy, which got him by when speaking to his superiors and the media, but it soon slipped back into hilarity when his guard was down addressing his juniors or losing his temper.

Milton entered the office tentatively. Deputy Assistant Commissioner Dobson was standing by the side of his desk with a familiar face sitting behind it.

"There is no need to introduce this gentleman to you now is there, John?" said Dobson, carefully trying not to miss his s's.

Facing Milton was Sir Michael Bryers, the Commissioner of the Metropolitan Police Force and the most powerful policeman in England.

"Take a seat, John," said the well-spoken Sir Michael, who cleared his throat as if preparing to make a long speech. Milton, who had not even spoken yet, knew what was coming.

Tapping the tips of his fingers from his left hand against those on his right just under his chin, Sir Michael continued, "Now, John, I received a phone call last night at 6.00 p.m. while I was enjoying a delightful fish supper with family friends. I don't like to be interrupted during supper at any time, so you can understand my annoyance at last night's little intrusion can't you, John?"

"Yes, sir," Milton replied with a slow blink and nod of the head while wishing this pompous twat would just get on with the rollicking.

Sir Michael continued, "The interruption came from the Home Secretary himself, who told me to switch on the television. What I saw almost made me choke on my salmon."

A pause followed as Sir Michael climbed up from behind the desk to walk towards the large window positioned directly behind it, which had a gorgeous glow coming through from the mid-morning sunshine.

Looking out onto the street below, Sir Michael proceeded, "Something tells me we are not on top of this situation. This hooliganism problem seems to be spiralling out of control. Now what I want to hear from you, John, is that this is not the case, that we have seen the last of the trouble and that England will gloriously win the bid for the 2006 World Cup and we will all live happily ever after."

A brief pause followed as Sir Michael turned his head towards Milton.

"If this is not the case ... then there will be a lot of people looking for a new job and I could well be forced to take early retirement and, believe me ..." He turned to face Milton. "... I am not ready for the pipe and slippers yet, young man!"

Milton, slightly bewildered as to how to reply, listened to Sir Michael's footsteps echo in the huge room as the Commissioner walked towards him and took his seat again.

"So then, John. Think, choose your words carefully and speak, but remember: there are a lot of heads on the chopping block and I have a wee tingling that the executioner's axe may well be getting sharpened as we speak."

For the first time, Milton realised fully that the blame for this mess so far went a lot further beyond him. He knew this was a national crisis, but for once it seemed that he was not the only person feeling the strain. Everyone was now feeling the pressure and he deduced - again for the first time - that a lot of people were relying on him, and he suddenly gained an added air of responsibility. For sure, he could end up being the scapegoat, but the fault for England not winning the World Cup bid due to mindless idiots causing trouble stretched all the way to the top; all the way to the Home Secretary at the very least.

"Well, sir," said Milton. "Our operation in Zurich was a massive success."

Expecting a roasting reply, he was surprised that both Sir Michael and Dobson were hanging on every word he said, although Dobson was very much Sir Michael's poodle and would not have dared speak first for fear of saying the wrong thing.

"We have arrested some prominent hooligans and we believe that we may have broken the back of the main ringleaders' chain. We have hundreds of hours of CCTV footage and expect to make some more arrests in the next fortnight."

Milton's momentum was snapped by a small, but deliberate, clearance of the throat from a member of his audience.

"Forgive me for interrupting," said Sir Michael whilst fingering a bound document on his lap. "But this seems to be the same terminology used in your last report. I think what you are reporting back to us is - excuse me for questioning - utter bollocks?"

There was a desperate silence as Milton wished the ground would open up below him and swallow him whole. Again Sir Michael left his seat and walked towards the window, brilliant sunshine now beaming into the room.

"I was a great friend of your father. You know that don't you, John?" The change of topic warmed Milton. "He was a brilliant policeman. Such a shame that he died in his prime. He had a heart of gold. Who would have thought it would have been that same heart that deprived the force of a sterling man?"

Sir Michael's address had suddenly become more personal, as if to bring a more familial feel to the discussion. It may also have been his clever way of eliciting a clear and truthful answer.

"I have followed your career, John, and I see a lot of your father in you. You are a fine policeman and you can produce results."

Then the Commissioner threw a curve ball that presented Milton with his first get-out clause since becoming entangled with this mess in the first place. Sir Michael rested his straight arms on the desk opposite Milton and leaned towards him.

"Yes or no, John? I want you to look me in the eye and tell me whether or not you can crack this or whether you want to stand down, walk away from it all and go back to your cushy job in the station."

Sir Michael walked over to the opposite side of the desk, next to Milton, rested his backside on the edge and repeated slowly, "Yes, or no, John?"

The mention of his father, a man he had idolised from the day he was born to the day he watched him draw his last breath, filled Milton with strength and a renewed thirst to succeed.

Milton looked straight back into the worried eyes of the Commissioner and with his clearest possible voice he announced with the confidence of an army colour sergeant on parade, "Yes, sir, I give you my word that we can still crack this."

* * *

"You and your good lady will have to come and taste my wife's delicious hotpots one of these nights, Steven," Sir Michael said to Dobson with a handshake.

As he popped his cap back on to return to the outside world, the Commissioner acknowledged Milton's confidence with a wink and a nod before shaking his hand and disappearing through the door.

Milton realised he had just received a rollicking and a rallying call at the same time and scratched his head at the bemusement of it all.

He felt warm inside because he had just received a vote of confidence from his most senior officer. But any confidence the Commissioner had instilled in him was soon undone by his immediate superior.

"You are one bloody lucky cookie, thunbeam," said Dobson almost as soon as the door closed behind the Commissioner. This time his lisp was as prominent as the shine from his bald head, freshly waxed that morning on the news that the Commissioner himself was to visit.

"If it wath left to me you would be out!" he shouted. "I don't give a damn who your dad wath and I thertainly don't give two flying fuckth about who the Commissioner thinkth YOU are! You are on your lath chanth Milton and if you threw up thith time, you will need Harry-bloody-Houdini to get you out of it!"

He gained his composure and continued his sermon methodically and lisp-free.

"I've always found you weak, Milton. This job was too big for you in the first place and I am being proved right now. What you don't seem to realise is that if you go down, we all go down. Do you realise what the World Cup being held in Britain will do for the nation? It could stop us sliding into recession. It is gold dust for us all, Milton, and we can't afford to let the bloody Germans steal it from under us. The country needs this. The Government needs this and even more importantly the people need this."

Milton could only deduce that the person who needed it most was the man preaching to him - Deputy Assistant Commissioner Dobson, who took a few deep breaths to calm down again and continued with his calm, professionally tuned, lispless accent.

"In two months' time England play in France, and then the following month England are in Germany. If the fans misbehave, we can all kiss goodbye to our pensions and you, my thon ..." The lisp returned. "... you can kith goodbye to everything becauth I will perthonally enthure that the ever-after in hell will theem like a holiday in paradith compared to what I will do to you."

Milton found a strange comfort in Dobson's ticking-off. His face had gone from pale to red as he struggled to suck in air quick enough to continue his barrage of abuse. His brow was damp and the drops of spit on Milton's jet black blazer showed that Dobson was firing more than verbal insults in his general direction.

After a brief pause, Milton hauled himself to his feet and with brave cynicism turned to his commanding officer and quipped, "Ith that all thir?"

Without even noticing the sarcasm, Dobson waved him away and Milton headed out through the heavy mahogany door.

He had not seen his wife for two weeks and decided he needed the rest of the day off. The debriefing with his officers could wait and the hours of CCTV viewing could begin without him.

It was time to return to the security of home and the loving arms of his Maggie. If there was ever a time when Milton needed his wife most, it was now. Worn out, defeated and feeling more alone than ever before in his life, Milton hailed a cab and was soon enveloped by the busy London traffic.

Chapter 3

Twenty-three Besworth Close had never looked so inviting - classic leafy suburbia and situated in a cul-de-sac idyllic for family life. The only problem for Milton was that in his pursuit of keeping everyone happy his anti-football hooliganism team had become more of a family than his actual family.

"That's twenty-seven quid, mate," stated the taxi driver, whose conversation all the way through London had centred on the crowd trouble he had witnessed the day before. He had drawn his own conclusion as to what should be done, not realising whom his fare payer was in the backseat.

"The cops have not got a clue, mate," he had declared. "They should just stop them travelling over. Lock up all the known troublemakers on the day of the game over here. There's no way they are going to get over there then, is there?"

Not wanting to be drawn into an argument, Milton had simply agreed and replied, "That's right, mate, lock the buggers up, although I think a few human rights organisations might have something to say about that."

"Bloody do-gooders, ruining the bloody country they are," he had growled over his shoulder.

The driver had then gone on to talk about his beloved Leyton Orient and how they would definitely go up that season and how they would become the Manchester United of the new millennium.

It made Milton realise just how much he actually hated the game and the lack of interest he had in it. Football had become his job, his life, but it was gradually strangling him every waking hour. Football was now England's official religion, and for the fans the World Cup 2006 would be the biggest religious festival the country would ever stage. Pilgrims would come from across the world to pay homage to a celebration of humanity. But to Milton it was still a bunch of overpaid playboys kicking a ball about a pitch.

Mind you, Milton had thought to himself, if people go to war over which God they follow, why shouldn't a few blokes have a punch-up over what colours they wear. It was all the same nonsense as far as he was concerned.

Suddenly he had found himself making excuses for football hooliganism. He smirked as the taxi pulled up to his semi-detached home.

"Keep the change, mate," he said, handing over three crisp ten pound notes. "And good luck for the season."

The taxi driver beamed like a Cheshire cat and shouted to the retreating Milton, "Hey, pal, you never said what colours you wear?"

Realising he didn't even support a football team, Milton stopped and turned with a grin. "The underdog, mate. I always put my money on the underdog!"

Milton quietly unlocked the light brown front door and sneaked into the carpeted hallway, the walls of which were adorned with family pictures.

It was almost two weeks since he had kissed Maggie and his two boys goodbye for a mission he was unable to tell them anything about. Milton may have been the head of the anti-hooliganism operation, but he was able to remain virtually anonymous, as his media-hungry superiors were glad to have their faces splashed across the morning papers. They had all expected early success and if the story finished with a happy ending they would be queuing up for the back slaps and the commendations. Meanwhile, the foot soldiers, marshalled by Milton, would be congratulated behind closed doors and promoted if they were lucky! They had even been termed internally as the 'stealth squad'.

None of this mattered to Milton anymore. He was determined not to fail and right now he just wanted to feel his Maggie's soft skin with his own fingertips, fill his nostrils with the fresh smell of her long brown hair and kiss those beautiful lips. He knew the kids would be at school so he could have an afternoon with his stunning wife of nine years.

The pair had met at a police function some 11 years earlier. Their fathers were friends and it seemed the perfect match that the offspring should tie the knot. Things had been going well, but the burden of the last 12 months had started to show. He couldn't remember the last time they had made love and Milton had spent more time in planes jetting around Europe than he had in his own front room with his family. Being unable to talk about his day's work made things even worse and more than once Maggie had suspected him of having an affair. Even his previous assignment undercover had been less of a burden on his private life.

However, he was going to brush all of his problems aside for the rest of that day and spend some long overdue quality time with his family. There was just one problem though. Milton's determination to surprise his wife meant that she did not know he would be home. On this particular Thursday afternoon, she had obviously decided to visit the gym, or a friend, or, as Milton shuddered to think, a lover.

Whatever. He decided he didn't want to waste the moment and went into the kitchen, freshly refurbished in that past year, to prepare a dinner to remember.

Two hours went by and Milton was still in the kitchen when he heard the front door open and in came Maggie. He rushed out and almost gave her a heart attack.

"My God, John. You almost killed me, you fool," she said.

Milton, unable to make out her beautiful facial features due to the glow from the sun that had entered the hallway with her, plunged for the outline.

"I've missed you, darling," he declared with a hug that lifted his wife off her feet. Without warning and not allowing her to speak by pressing his lips firmly against hers, he carried her up the 16 stairs to the bedroom and closed the door.

"John, this can't go on," Maggie said, breaking the silence, as the two lay naked on the thick quilted bed.

"This is not a proper marriage. I've seen Lord Lucan more times than I've seen you over the past year. The kids miss you but most of all, John, I miss you. I miss having my husband."

It struck a chord with Milton. "I understand, honey, but it will all be over soon, don't worry. At the most, I have three months of this mess remaining and then it is all over."

"Three months, John! Three months! I'm not sure if I can go on like this for another three months. Not knowing if you are coming home at night. Not even knowing if you are in the same country as us. In three months, John, you might come home but don't be surprised if there's no one here to greet you."

Maggie, understandably upset, climbed off the bed and wrapped her dressing gown around her well-trimmed body.

Milton pulled on a pair of jogging shorts and sat at the end of the bed to listen to more from his wife.

"What am I supposed to say to people who ask what you are up to, John?" she continued. "I was having coffee this morning with Janet and Ellie and both were asking if you had left me because you have hardly been around. Do you know how that makes me feel?"

Milton had had enough of the verbal battering and decided it was time to defend himself.

"Janet and Ellie's husbands are bankers. I am a Detective Inspector with the Metropolitan Police Force. I am seconded to special duties and I am pushing myself to the sodding limit trying to keep everybody happy. Has anyone for a minute stopped to ask how I feel about things?"

The increase in volume told Maggie that her husband was sincere. She tried to interrupt but he got in first.

"I would be quite happy being a desk sergeant in some shitty village police station, but no, everybody expects me to be just like my father, just like your father and no one is worse for this than you, Maggie. I am trying to secure a future for us all here and I would like a bit of support." There was a brief pause. "PLEASE?"

The argument was halted by a bang on the front door, which was still ajar, and an inquisitive yell of "hello?" from the hallway.

"Shit, that's Janet," said Maggie. "It was her turn to pick up the boys after school."

The pair ran down the stairs, Milton still in his shorts and Maggie desperately trying to tie the belt to her dressing gown before she came into view of the front door. Janet's sly smile told Milton and Maggie that it was perfectly obvious what they had been up to.

"Good to see you back, John," said Janet. "Maggie's missed you."

This was followed by simultaneous infant shouts of "daddy, daddy" from two gloriously blond-haired boys running from the Ford Focus parked on the pavement outside.

"Hi boys! Daddy's missed you so much and I've cooked us all a lovely dinner to make up for not seeing you for a couple of weeks."

Milton turned to enter the living room carrying five-year-old John jnr and holding the hand of seven-year-old Jack.

The girls exchanged smiles at the door and Maggie pivoted to enjoy the first family moment they had shared for some time. She was feeling lonely, but never in her mind had she ever thought of leaving her husband. How would she explain that to her friends and how would it go down with her parents? No, John was a good man. It was just a shame he was never around.

The rest of the afternoon was spent painting, drawing, watching the television cartoons and generally being a proper family. There were smiles all round - if only life could be like that every day.

"Come on, kids, it's time to eat," said Maggie, who had decided to trash her husband's sad effort of a roast dinner after smoke from the oven filled the kitchen. So she had whipped up a quick spag. bol. instead.

The two boys gulped down their small portions and returned to the television, leaving the couple with a few minutes to themselves.

"I'm sorry, honey, about earlier," apologised Maggie. "I just listened to too many other people and let it all build up inside. I love you, John, but I want you closer to the kids and me. Dad said that by the time he was your age he was being lined up as a Commissioner. He said he never spent so much time away from his family. Surely you must be close to that by now?"

This was a conversation Milton had been through a thousand times. It was beginning to wear thin.

"Honey, the force has changed since your father's day. You don't just solve a few burglaries to climb up the promotion ladder anymore.

"I promise that after this one I will take a desk job and work 9 til 5 if that is what you want. I promise. I just need your support. At least give me that, Maggie, because at the moment I don't seem to have anyone on my side.

"I am walking up a hill backwards. It's taking me ages to get to the top of this case and I don't know what I will find when I get there. At the same time I'm looking down at what I'm leaving behind and every day it is becoming more tempting just to walk back down the hill because at least I can see what is down there.

"If I do that though, honey, we can kiss goodbye to all this and I will have to start again. That's the last thing any of us want now isn't it?"

Maggie reluctantly agreed but it was not what she wanted to hear. She wanted to brag over an oversized Costa Coffee mug to her friends that her husband was going places and they would be moving to their five-bedroom detached house soon. After what her husband had just announced, this now all seemed a distant dream.

The kids were packed off to bed and an exhausted Milton and Maggie called it a night early. They made love again before falling asleep but both had very different things on their minds this time. Earlier that afternoon it was raw, exciting sex, like teenagers discovering each other for the first time once again. This time it was more disciplined, going through the motions like a married couple of nine years. If they had been able to read each other's minds they would probably have stopped halfway through.

Maggie was desperately trying to work out what she was going to say to her friends over coffee the next morning. "Oh, we had a wonderful day but I'm not sure when I will see him next." This would only add fuel to the speculation that they were close to splitting up. She hated being the topic of their rumour-mongering.

Milton, on the other hand, had a totally different agenda. Ahead of him lay hours of watching CCTV footage and looking for a breakthrough that could bring an end to all this nonsense and let him return to being a normal husband, if there could be such a thing for a policeman working undercover.

Chapter 4

The drive to work the next morning gave Milton plenty of time to contemplate his predicament.

"Will you be home this weekend?" was the last thing Maggie had said to him on the doorstep.

"I'll call you later," was the only reply he could muster.

He felt that his wife was falling out of love with him. Or, more likely, falling out of love with the situation she was in.

In the first eight years of their marriage, Maggie was partnered with a high flyer in the Metropolitan Police Force, a man being groomed for the higher echelons, and she had bragged to her jealous friends until their coffees went cold. Now her friends were getting their own back. Detecting all was not well in the Milton household, they were quick to pounce, messing with Maggie's mind and making her believe that her husband was more interested in his job than his family.

Milton's quest to please everyone else had started to backfire badly and he would be the first to admit that his current assignment had made him selfish and insular. He was desperate to succeed now, and if his wife was getting fed up then so be it. If she couldn't wait the few months more that he needed to get on top of this case, then maybe he was better off without her. He was beginning to resent his lack of support from those closest to him. The fact that he could never tell his own wife what he was actually working on had not helped the situation at all.

The job was taking over his life and the only way he could get his life back would be by cracking the case: bring the ringleaders to justice and ensure the World Cup came to England in 2006. The irony of it all, as he smirked to himself, was that such was his distaste for football that he probably wouldn't bother watching a single match even if he were given free tickets to the World Cup Final itself.

The crawl through the London Friday morning traffic meant that he reached his office some time after his team, who, to their credit, were still remarkably keen despite the lack of progress.

The unit had their own central London offices: six rooms in all, containing the latest television and computer technology that Japan was able to manufacture. There had been no expense spared in the British Government's bid to catch the thugs, and this had made Milton's excuses even harder for his superiors to swallow.

"Morning troops," Milton announced as he entered the video analysis room, removing his jacket and throwing it over an empty chair.

"Morning sir," was the reply in unison from four junior officers who had already started wading through the CCTV footage gathered from Zurich city centre and the other main areas affected by the trouble two days earlier.

He picked up a memo, which had been neatly folded and placed into his pigeonhole. It was from the public relations department and stated that *The Sun* newspaper would like ten clear images to splash over its front page and centre pages as their bid to 'back our bobbies' in catching the yobs. He handed it to one of his officers to deal with and walked over to the screens.

"What have we got, Waite?" Milton enquired of his eager sergeant in whom he placed the most faith. They were all good officers, but Waite stood out.

"Well sir, it seems to be the same story as the last match," Waite replied, lifting himself out of his office chair. "You see this screen? This is where most of the arrested fans that we interrogated claimed the trouble started, and yet nothing is captured on film. It looks perfectly peaceful." Pointing at three other screens he added, "And, as you can see, this is where it escalated to."

The screens showed madness, terror, insanity. Men punching, kicking, smashing and people running here, there and everywhere. Absolute mayhem.

"Sir, it just doesn't make sense," continued Waite. "If I rewind the tapes, you can see that the trouble spills out from this area here." He again pointed to the screens at what looked like a normal day with empty streets.

"Are you sure you have the correct order of footage, Waite?" asked Milton.

"Definitely, sir. I walked that area of town with you a hundred times last week. It just doesn't make sense."

Waite was right. Milton wheeled away to absorb the scenario. The time and the location that the cameras were covering should have revealed how the trouble started and yet the street was empty, with not even a stray dog or discarded paper blowing in the wind.

Then Milton thought back to John Simons - the thug that they questioned back at the temporary lock-up in Zurich. He declared that the men he believed started the trouble looked to be well organised and trained. The officers confirmed that it had become a common sentiment among the arrested fans.

Rubbing his hand on the back of his neck, Milton returned for a closer look at the screens and then turned to face his team.

"Let me throw something at you guys. Don't interrupt me, just hear me out.

"Let's just say that, somehow, someone has managed to get to these cameras; doctor them in some way in order to conceal their identities and then managed to restore them before we got to the cameras the following morning."

His troops looked at him puzzled, but did not interrupt. Any new theory or line of investigation was welcome at that point.

"Okay, let me take it a bit further." Milton patrolled the room. "We have been looking for troublemakers - drunks, yobs, street fighters - and we have arrested hundreds of them over the past year. And yet the trouble persists and, let's be honest about it, it's getting worse. Something tells me that we have been targeting the wrong sort of villain.

"As time has been ticking on, we have been targeting amateurs when we should have been looking for professionals. Let's face it, the force wasn't looking for pickpockets after the Brinks Matt gold robbery and the scale of this violence is the same. We are simply wasting our time and resources even talking to most of the idiots arrested in Zurich, just like the other matches we have investigated."

Milton's Sherlock Holmes-like address was stopped in its tracks by an abrupt "sir" shouted by Sergeant Sandra Bennett.

As Milton turned, she was pointing at one of the screens they had been observing. Milton walked closer to the screen and leaned over Bennett's shoulder as a smile started to stretch across his face.

"Well, will you look at that?" Milton whispered into Bennett's ear before proclaiming, "Houston, we have made contact!"

Milton edged even closer to the screen, which had earlier displayed an empty street next to the one onto which the trouble had spilled. Now, though, he could just make out on the right-hand side of the screen some sort of commotion.

It was obvious to Milton what had happened. Someone had taken a photograph of the scene from the exact position of the camera and somehow positioned it in front to show that same constant image. However, the picture had slipped to the left slightly and was revealing the truth as to what had actually taken place two days earlier in that particular part of Zurich.

Although difficult to make out in the small corner of the screen not covered by the photograph, Milton could see punches being thrown, plenty of white England shirts and what looked like a fight escalating into something bigger; something the whole world was able to hear about on their 9.00 o'clock news programmes.

Suddenly one thing stood out on the screen more than anything. He focused his laser-like gaze as if spotting a pound coin on the floor of a busy pub.

"Stop it there, Waite. Rewind a fraction and blow it up to full screen."

The keen sergeant did as he was told.

"Okay, play it from there in slow motion," ordered Milton.

What they could make out on the grainy screen was a man in a black shirt performing what looked like the tail end of a fight manoeuvre that was certainly not beer-induced. It left its audience watching open-jawed.

"Has anyone seen our pathetic bunch of beer-bellied maulers do anything like this before?" asked Milton to no one in particular as he took charge of Waite's control panel to rewind the tape again. They watched as the man blocked what looked like a punch and sent his rival crashing to the ground with a kick normally reserved for martial arts movies.

Unfortunately for Milton, at no point was the man's face visible, but nevertheless he ordered Waite to sharpen the image and produce as large a printout as possible of the man's head.

The printer seemed to take forever as it spewed out the image taken from a back-sided angle.

Milton grabbed it from the printer and was dumbstruck by what he saw.

Tucked in the man's ear was what appeared to be some sort of earplug. Milton would have liked to believe that this man had an ear infection of some kind, but having seen the karate-style move moments earlier he suspected different.

This man was wearing some sort of communications device. He was receiving orders. This was all going in a horribly wrong new direction and Milton felt as if he had just been punched in the stomach and had to sit down.

Moments earlier he was asking his officers to believe his own theory of a professional unit orchestrating England's football violence, and now he had possible proof, even he found it hard to swallow.

"People," he announced from his chair. "We have been hunting in the wrong river. It seems to me, after looking at what we have here, that there is a great white calling the shots out there and we have just wasted the last 12 months fishing for bloody tiddlers."

Milton had mixed feelings about what he had uncovered. Sure, this could now explain why the trouble was happening time and time again. But once again the same questions had to be asked: who are they, where are they and, more importantly, what the hell are they?

Nevertheless, it was a breakthrough and the next few hours were spent trying to find more CCTV images of men who fought more like trained assassins than football louts. The footage from the city centre was inconclusive.

The Sun would have more than its ten pictures to choose from for its weekend edition, but even the arrest of these men would not make an ounce of difference to solving the problem. As Milton had discovered with previous matches, there were plenty of new recruits willing to take the place of those arrested, but it was the men at the top who mattered most and, apart from the brief glimpse captured earlier that morning, the day looked like finishing with nothing more.

"Okay, folks, let's get our thinking caps on." Milton broke a silence that had lasted for hours as the unit got stuck into its collective job.

"Think, people, think. Think back to all the other matches we've done. Copenhagen, Rome, Warsaw, Madrid. At any time have any of you come across anything like this?"

He again held up the picture of the karate kid with the earplug. "Waite, you took a team undercover in Warsaw, you must have seen characters like this? Professionals? Anyone you thought was calling the shots?"

Waite shook his head. He was reminiscing about the time he had travelled abroad five months earlier with two other undercover officers and had ended up sucking his meals through a straw for a fortnight after breaking his jaw. The well-built Waite had been recognised in a bar by a hooligan from his home manor of Tottenham and had received a kicking he would not forget in a hurry, along with his two colleagues.

"Sir, I would rather not remember that trip!"

His reply was met by sympathetic sniggers from his colleagues. One of the men was still off work with a fractured skull, such was the ferocity of the attack. Since then, Milton had deemed it too dangerous to send in undercover police until they had a strong enough lead to go in for the kill. Maybe now that moment was approaching, only this time he knew he wanted a slice of the action himself.

"Okay, guys," Milton readdressed his weary troops. "I know it's been a hard few weeks but I feel we are close to catching something big; something that could provide us with our first genuine lead. I can't force you to, but I ask you. Please work with me this weekend in going over these tapes again because I seriously believe something will fall onto our laps from this."

The four officers present had not taken a day off for almost three weeks and were approaching the end of their tether. At 4.30 p.m. on a Friday, Milton expected them all to get up and walk out of the door, but was astonished by the show of solidarity.

"We're in this with you, guv," said Waite, who was backed up by words and nods of agreement from the three other officers.

Milton was a likeable man and had won the respect of his comrades. They, like him, had lived through this over the past year and maybe sensed too that they were close to something big. Milton felt a lump in his throat as he ordered, "Back to work," and rolled up his sleeves for the long night ahead.

Milton couldn't remember if it was 4.00 or 5.00 a.m. when he had last looked at his clock, but he was awoken at his desk by Sergeant Bennett who walked in with a tray of toast and tea.

"Morning fellas," she announced. "It's 10.00 a.m. and time for breakfast."

The officers were strewn around the room like the remnants of a student party and started stretching their arms and rubbing their eyes as they tucked into the pyramid of toast.

Milton was somewhat disappointed with himself, and not just for having fallen asleep. He remembered, firstly, that he had forgotten to call Maggie and, secondly, that his team had failed to find anything other than the karate kid footage from earlier on.

"I must have looked at these damn tapes ten times last night," Waite declared while throwing a VHS onto his desk. "I'm going to get square eyes if I look at these screens much longer."

In response, Sergeant Bennett, a slightly butch and yet attractive 31-year-old, quipped, "Better than the cross eyes you've got from spanking your monkey three times a day!"

The injection of humour made Milton feel good and it showed that his team had established a remarkable sense of camaraderie since coming together.

"I think we've seen enough of the shopping centre footage, Waite. Let's start having a look at the football ground stuff. After all, it is Saturday and Saturday's a day for watching football, right?"

Milton's attempt at humour wasn't a touch on Bennett's earlier jape and he decided that maybe he should leave the funnies to his juniors.

The day progressed. The team reached the end of the tapes and, despite a few isolated incidents, there was no sign of anything resembling the breakthrough they caught the previous day.

They had routinely focused on recognising faces, identifying familiar faces and known names to try to piece together the sequence back through the running battles in order to locate its source. But they had not looked for the unlikely, which only the sharp eyes of the boss were doing.

"Waite!" Milton called his junior over.

Milton was watching the generic views of a camera showing a wide shot of the shopping precinct, which had been the epicentre of the lunchtime trouble.

"What's that?" he asked Waite, pointing to a dark smudge hovering in the distance.

"That's a helicopter, sir. I didn't realise we had aerial surveillance this time, sir," replied Waite, recalling their actions the previous week.

"Exactly. It must be the Swiss Police or TV. Get on the blower, Waite, and tell them we need all the footage they shot from that chopper."

Waite scurried off through the door and into one of the adjoining offices as Milton sat and stared at the screen.

After what seemed like an eternity, but which was probably only ten minutes, Waite returned.

"Sir, the Swiss said they didn't have a chopper in the sky on that day and the only aerial footage that the TV shot was during the game itself, from 8.00 p.m. onwards."

Pointing at the security camera's recorded time in the bottom right-hand corner of the screen, Waite said, "This was taken at noon during the trouble.

"Okay, Waite, work your magic on this image and give me a good printout of this chopper," said Milton, who sensed he may be onto something.

As Waite brought the black blur to life, white writing started to appear along the tail of the chopper.

Milton waited patiently by the printer, but inside he felt like a kid on Christmas morning eager to open his presents.

As the printer churned out the image, he was able to read the writing on the side of the helicopter as clear as day.

"Alpine Tours."

A thousand theories buzzed around Milton's head, but he asked himself just loud enough for everyone present to hear, "Why on earth would anyone want to take an aerial city tour when the beautiful Alps are only a stone's throw away?"

Again his gut feeling told him that he might have made another key breakthrough. The helicopter appeared to be hovering above the vicinity of the trouble, and if it wasn't the police or the media, then who was it?

"Waite, I want you to get the Swiss onto this and find out exactly who hired this chopper on that day. Let's call it a day, folks. Enjoy what's left of your weekend and I'll see you back here on Monday morning - 8.00 a.m. sharp!"

Milton charged out of the door and knew he had just rewarded himself and his team with a day off.

Saturday was fast disappearing, but he could spend all of Sunday with his family with a clear head. Maybe the park, maybe the swimming baths or maybe the swings and slides?

Whatever he did, he had not felt this good in months, and he made his way homewards across London as fast as his Audi A8 and the heavy traffic would allow.

Chapter 5

Milton's elation at his first productive day's work for some time was soon dampened when he arrived home. The house was empty and looked like it had been empty all day. The note on the kitchen table explained it all:

"Hi honey, on the off-chance that you may come home, me and the kids have gone camping down south for the weekend with the Thompsons. We didn't want to sit in all weekend hoping that you might at least call. The weather isn't always like this in September so we decided to make the most of it. We'll be travelling back early Monday in time for the kids to get to school."

The footnote summed up his wife's frame of mind:

"In the likelihood that you don't read this, John. ... Hi Maggie, he's done it to you again, another weekend on your own!"

Once again Milton was alone. Should he drive down to Brighton? Should he catch up and play dad? Was it even Brighton they had gone to? He had a free Saturday night for once and he was all dressed up with no place to go.

"Shit!" he whispered to himself as he crumpled up the note and threw it unsuccessfully towards the dustbin.

He grabbed a bottle of beer out of the fridge, headed for one of the two easy chairs in the living room and flicked the 'on' button on the remote control.

BBC News was harping on about the aftermath of the violence earlier in the week. British politicians, British ex-players, German politicians, German ex-players all had their say.

Sod it, Milton thought to himself. Why should I waste my first Saturday night off in ages? I'm heading to the pub.

He was doing this more to spite his wife than to satisfy himself.

As a teenager, he was a bit of a hellraiser. He could turn a woman's head in his day and, at 32, he was still relatively good looking despite the stresses of his current predicament taking their toll on his features.

He had forgotten what it was like to let what was left of his hair down and tonight he was determined to go and enjoy a few pints down the local with the boys. But none of the boys would be there waiting for him. His healthy group of mates from his younger years had long forgotten about Milton, who had deserted them for his wife and his career at a time when they were still enjoying nights out and meeting new birds.

His social life was as non-existent as his married life, but a couple of pints of Guinness was exactly what he needed right now as he left the loneliness of his family home and headed off to the pub.

* * *

The phone ring sounded more like an air raid siren as Milton refused to open his eyes to unleash a pounding headache. His two pints of Guinness had turned into seven and it was probably the first time he had drunk that much since his stag night. He had enjoyed his night of freedom a little too much and was going to pay the consequences for the rest of the day. Dealing with hangovers was not his field of expertise.

"Hello?" he answered the phone with a gruff voice, hoping it would be Maggie on the other end.

"Guv?" enquired the voice at the other end, which sounded distinctly like Waite.

"What time is it, Sergeant?" he asked, expecting it still to be the middle of the night.

"Just gone 11 sir?"

"Is that a.m. or p.m.?"

Waite laughed and concluded, "Sounds like someone has had a good night!"

Milton propped himself upright, realising that the call must be of some importance.

"Fire away, Waite. What do you want?"

"Sir, I've heard back from the Swiss about the chopper. I'll meet you at the office in an hour. This is going to blow you away, sir."

"Will do Waite … and Waite, this better be good because you are interrupting a perfectly good hangover!"

Waite replied with a laugh, which was followed by the tone of a dead line. Without even hanging up, Milton let himself fall back onto his pillow with a thud and a groan.

Milton was at the office long before the hour was up. After throwing up what looked like most of the Guinness and the Chinese takeaway he had bought on the way home, he showered, sunk a pint of water accompanied by two Anadins and set off in a morning-after daze into London.

Waite was there already with a faxed piece of A4 in his hand.

"Sir, you are not going to believe this. We have turned over a whole new leaf in this saga and it is going to give you a hell of a shock."

"Waite, if you don't cut the crap and get to the chase soon, you are not going to believe what I will do with this pencil!" Milton gestured by pointing the sharp end towards Waite.

"Sorry, sir."

He took a deep breath and continued.

"The helicopter was chartered on the day of the game by three men who also chartered the same chopper two weeks earlier."

"Three men?" Milton pondered, as his sergeant was about to carry on with his mouth gawping. "Sorry, carry on, Waite."

"The Swiss have questioned the owner of the chopper who said that the same three men came on both occasions. Two were qualified helicopter pilots with British military experience and produced the documentation to allow them to take the chopper up for the day.

"Now, on the first occasion, the men produced cash to hire the chopper and also paid the £5,000 security deposit in cash up front. But here is the chestnut: on the second occasion, on the day of the game, they again paid for the rental of the chopper in cash, but apparently they did not have the cash for the deposit. The owner said there was some debate because the men argued amongst themselves for a while and then reluctantly handed over a credit card for the owner to swipe."

On mentioning this, Waite waved the piece of A4 in the air.

"The owner, suspicious of the men's reluctance to let him have any identification documents, took a photocopy of the credit card before he ripped up the swipe he took from it on safe return of the chopper."

Milton took the paper from Waite's fingers and staring back at him was the name Carson Jacks.

"What else did the owner say about these men, Waite?"

"He said they were definitely English with athletic builds and, for some reason, he said the most striking feature of all three was their suntans!"

"What do you mean suntan?"

"Well, he said they were definitely English but looked as though they lived on the Med or something. It was like one of those ..." Waite checked his notes sent through from Switzerland. "... year-round tans."

Milton stared down at the credit card details and another piece of the puzzle fell into place in his mind.

At the top of the card was scribbled writing that looked like Arabic and underneath was the English translation: The National Bank of Dubai.

"Oh my God, Waite," exclaimed Milton as he dropped the hand clutching the sheet to his side and walked towards the window. "What the hell have we stumbled across now? How far wide of the mark have we been? How many people do you know living on the Med that have a Dubai credit card?"

Giving himself a moment to gather his thoughts, Milton ordered Waite to run the name Carson Jacks through every computer database available.

"I want to know everything there is on this man Carson Jacks. This could be the spark that lights the fire, my man. Something tells me our adventure has just begun," he said to Waite.

Little did he know how right he was.

Chapter 6

Carson Jacks, it appeared, was somewhat of an unknown quantity.

Neither Scotland Yard nor Interpol had any records of him and a search of police and local council records the length and breadth of the country also failed to throw any light on the character who had now become the focal point of Milton's investigations.

Each day for the week following the discovery of this vital name had uncovered more frustrations and it seemed that Carson Jacks was the proverbial invisible man.

It seemed that the only way they were going to find out who this man really was would be via information received from the Dubai Police Force with whom Milton's unit had established contact.

"Okay, so what do we have, people?" said Milton at the daily morning briefing the following Friday, some six days after first coming across the name Carson Jacks.

"Well, sir, nothing with the DVLA," said Sergeant Bennett. "They have a record of a Carson Jacks, but he is 72 and lives in Cleethorpes. We checked him out just in case, but he has not left the country in three years. The last time was to go to France on a weekend visit.

"We have also run checks through the tax office, local councils and even the Home Office records and criminal system. Nothing, sir."

"Great! That just about dries up all the avenues in this country. What has the local force in Dubai told us, Waite?" He turned to his number one deputy.

"It's not easy, sir. They have been very slow coming back to me," he replied.

"What do you mean slow getting back to you? I only want them to run a check on this man's credit card." Milton was getting agitated.

"You don't understand, guv. I am dealing with a Captain Ali and I must have rung him up at least 60 times this week. He's either on his break, is busy or has gone to the mosque. He knows how urgent it is, but he keeps telling me he has to go through his superior and when I ask him what the hold-up is he says his boss is ..."

Waite paused, much to the annoyance of Milton.

"Yes, Waite? And?"

"Well, he says his boss is either on a break, is busy or has gone to the mosque."

The reply was met by Milton banging a clenched fist against his own forehead in disbelief.

"Waite, this is the only lead we have on one of the biggest criminal cases that this country has ever investigated. I want you to get on that phone to Captain Ali now and tell him we need information today or we will go directly over his head and leave him in the biggest pile of shit he could ever imagine. My God, Waite, it would be quicker if I went over there and got the information myself."

His last comment left him thinking how realistic a suggestion that actually was. Surely it wouldn't be such a bad idea to fly to Dubai and sniff around. At least it would get him out of his shitty little world for a while. Where is Dubai anyway? Saudi Arabia? he thought to himself, 'Don't they cut your hand off for picking your nose over there?'

"Sir," Waite continued, "I can't ring him up today."

"Why the hell not?"

"Today is Friday and Friday is the Muslim holy day of rest. There's no one working over there," he explained.

"For God's sake!" exclaimed Milton, wondering if it could get any worse. "Ring him on his mobile! I want results by the end of the day, people, otherwise we are all in over the weekend."

Waite knew everyone's weekend plans relied on his being able to get hold of the elusive Captain Ali. Maybe he should just make up some bogus information? Surely someone in Dubai couldn't be connected to this spate of football violence across Europe, could they? Waite's mind raced.

But Waite was a first-class copper and his professional integrity forced him to try that Dubai dialing code one more time.

"Hello? Captain Ali?" asked a shocked Waite, who expected his efforts to be met by: "Sorry but the mobile phone you are trying to connect with has been switched off ..."

"Aaaaaahhhhhh, my beautiful friend from England, Sergeant Waite, no?" was the reply.

"Hello Captain Ali, how are you today, sir?" asked Waite in slow easy-to-understand English.

"Very well, Sergeant Waite. The sun is shining, the sky is clear and God is great. Everything is beautiful!"

Waite realised quickly that beautiful was obviously the new word Captain Ali had learned that week.

"Sir, I have been trying to get through to you over the last two days but you haven't returned my calls," he said.

"Oh, I am sorry. I had no record of your calling. You know, Sergeant, sometimes messages just don't get through here. How can I help you now?"

"I am still awaiting information on a Carson Jacks, the man I contacted you about earlier this week."

Judging by his progress to date, Waite felt like he had been dealing with an incompetent idiot but was pleasantly surprised by the Captain's reply.

"I have plenty of information you require. I have just been waiting for you to call me and to let me know where you want it sending."

The discussion could have gone around in circles all day but at least Waite could see a weekend out of the office in sight.

"Fantastic, Captain Ali. I need you to fax it to me urgently on this number … have you got a pen?"

Waite reeled off the control room's number complete with international dialing code.

"Okay, I have the number. I will send you the information tomorrow, In sha'Allah," added Captain Ali.

Waite had learned that 'In sha'Allah' is the Arabic way of saying, "You'll get it when you get it." Waite had heard it plenty of times before and voiced his concern.

"Captain Ali, I cannot stress enough the importance of receiving this information straight away. I plead with you to send it through today," he remonstrated.

"My dear Sergeant, today is Friday. It is our day of rest. I will send it through tomorrow."

"Sir, I beg you. Please send it through today. I will be forever in your debt," pleaded Waite, who had the distinct impression after his lack of progress over the past week that every day was a day of rest in Dubai. Playing the Arabs at their own game seemed to have struck a chord though.

"You sound like a desperate man. You have my word that I will fax your information through, how do you say it in England, AASP?"

"That's ASAP," corrected Waite. "You don't know how grateful I am that you're doing this."

Waite decided not to report the news to Milton due to his let-downs throughout the week from Dubai, but instead sat tight with his fingers crossed and his eyes glued to the fax machine.

Two hours later the fax machine rang and Waite jumped to his feet and ran over - the third time he had done this in the past hour.

"Waiting for something important?" Sergeant Bennett asked inquisitively. "One thing's for sure, it won't be a love letter!"

The top of the first piece of paper showed Arabic writing and Waite blurted out "Yes!" and clenched his fist close to his chest. "Sir, we've got the stuff coming through from Dubai."

Milton joined Waite by the fax machine as three pieces of A4 spewed out.

The first displayed Jacks's bank details, which showed that he had held a current account with the National Bank of Dubai since 1992. It had a healthy balance and revealed that he had no outstanding loans.

The second was a copy of his Dubai driving licence, again issued in 1992, which was clean and contained a clear photograph of a 33-year-old man. His age was given away by the date of birth on the credit-card-sized licence.

The third was a copy of a certificate, but it was entirely in Arabic. Luckily, Captain Ali had summarised what it said.

"My butiful Sergeant Waite," beautiful being spelt horrendously wrong. "It appears that your Carson Jacks is what we call a VIP resident of Dubai. This is a copy of his residency certificate and it shows that he is sponsored by the local ruling family.

"He is a managing director of a company called Expatriatedotcom, which is an Internet mail-order company selling patriotic items online. You know, flags, mugs, t-shirts, etc., with countries' flags on. It is based in Dubai and currently employs around 50 men, all from the UK. Hope this is of some use. Your friend, Ali Yousef."

At that moment, Milton could have kissed Captain Ali Yousef and declared lifelong love for his Arab counterpart.

The sense of relief could be felt across the room as Milton patrolled it like a robot on speed. His excitement could not be contained.

"Yes, yes, yes, yes, yes!" he declared as he slapped high fives with each member present.

"After 12 months of running up dark alleys, there is some light at the end of the tunnel at last," he said.

Announcing that everyone could report back on Monday, he headed across the centre of London to report his findings to Dobson and he couldn't care less if his lisping boss did cover him in spit. At last he had something positive to report and he knew he was going to be jetting off to the sun as soon as his boss allowed it.

Milton's excitement during the mobile phone call he made to Dobson on his way across London obviously set his boss's pulse running, for when Milton arrived at the office Sir Michael was also there along with a number of other senior officers from the force.

Milton then proceeded with his theory.

He explained about the doctored CCTV camera and about what looked like a professionally trained man fighting, with the communication device tucked in his ear. He seemed to get the most attention when he mentioned the helicopter, which had been hired by a Carson Jacks, one of three Englishmen with a 'year-round suntan'.

His theory was that, for some reason, the Dubai-based company, Expatriatedotcom, was connected with all the football trouble. Thus, to stop the violence, someone needed to go in and find out why. That someone, Milton concluded and presented, was himself.

Milton was asked to leave the room while his proposal was discussed.

Leaning against the wall in the hallway, he had it all mapped out in his mind. He would travel to Dubai, befriend Carson Jacks or one of his henchmen and find out what the hell was going on.

He had done undercover surveillance work before, but not on this case. Eighteen months earlier, he had worked as a drugs dealer for nine weeks in order to crack one of the biggest cartels operating in South London.

He was convincing. He lived the life of a dealer and even grew to enjoy it. At one stage, his commanding officer at the time threatened to take him off the job because they thought he was becoming too involved. The job saw the life of his undercover partner taken. His throat was slit by a drug addict who was desperate for a fix despite having no cash.

This made Milton even more determined and he eventually succeeded in bringing seven men to book and smashing an international multimillion pound empire. One was jailed for life for a string of drug-related murders.

Milton's reward was a notch up the promotional ladder and the anti-hooliganism task force assignment.

An hour passed before he was called back in.

"Well, John," said the well-spoken Sir Michael, "we are delighted with this breakthrough and we have decided to give you complete control over whatever course of action you decide to take."

The length of the discussion and the glares he was receiving from Dobson told him that not everyone was in agreement with this, but he couldn't give a toss. He had received another vote of confidence from Sir Michael and he wasn't going to let him down.

"Thank you, sir," he said in acknowledgement as Sir Michael concluded, "I believe you will need some suncream. Dubai can be frightfully hot at this time of year."

Chapter 7

Milton had 24 hours from the time he was given the green light to the time that he actually climbed on board his Emirates flight from Heathrow bound for Dubai.

He had the bit between his teeth now and was confident of a fruitful trip. His wife had not seen it that way, of course.

Maggie was still completely oblivious to what case Milton was actually working on. So when he was packing his case and turned to tell her he would be gone for some time, it sparked a barrage of abuse from her. She was hysterical and it underlined the fact that their marriage was now under severe strain.

Milton stressed that this would be the very last mission, but he had told her that before. This time he honestly meant it, but how could he get it across to someone who was quite simply sick of his absence from the family house?

He had kissed her on the forehead before rushing out to his airport pick-up, which was provided by Waite, but deep down Milton also knew that the Dubai connection gave him a great excuse to get away from everything - and that included the mundane family life that he had honestly begun to despise.

"You know, Waite, the last thing you should do is get married," he said, jumping into the front seat. "I think they should make it illegal for any man under the age of 50 to marry. Believe me, it would save people one hell of a lot of trouble!"

His two-hour wait in the departure lounge allowed him to read up on Dubai, which to his surprise was not in Saudi Arabia but the United Arab Emirates. This was a relief to Milton, who really was going in blind. He was also delighted to read that in September the temperature would be touching the 100-degree mark and that Dubai was one of the fastest-growing tourism destinations in the world.

He read that there were beaches, nightlife, booze and a five-star cosmopolitan lifestyle. In addition, he was informed by a young man sitting next to him who was also travelling to Dubai that over 4,000 young expatriate women working for Emirates Airline lived there.

Suddenly this wasn't looking like such a tough assignment after all.

But the sobering thoughts of his current scenario and the mission at hand saw the bronze beaches of the holiday brochures and the thought of nights on the town with blonde-haired trolley dollies pale into insignificance.

Here he was. One man with the weight of a country's expectations on his shoulders. He realised how Tim Henman must feel each year at Wimbledon.

He was unable to sleep on the flight over. Instead he continued to wise up on his destination and watched a couple of movies that he would never have had the chance to see at the cinema. He could not even remember the last time he had actually been to the cinema; probably during those early exciting years of marriage.

The seven-hour flight crossed Europe and the Levant before the on-board map showed that he was flying over the Arabian Gulf and was within an hour of touchdown. He started to feel nervous. He really did not know what to expect.

Administration had sorted out some hotel accommodation for a couple of nights, but he really would need to slip into the expatriate lifestyle as soon as possible if he were to have any chance of infiltrating the operations of Jacks and his merry men.

He had convinced himself that Jacks was responsible. Of course he had never been caught. Flying in from the Middle East, he would have slipped in and out under the hooligan radar without anyone raising an eyebrow.

Milton had only ever instructed host countries to check manifests of flights arriving from England. Border checks were carried out to ensure that known hooligans weren't flying into neighbouring countries and then hopping over the border. Never had he thought it necessary to check flights coming in from places like the Middle East. But it was starting to make sense.

What didn't make sense, however, was why they were doing it and why members of his group had never been caught at any previous matches. This was going to be a tough nut to crack, but time was running out and Milton knew he was taking the biggest gamble of his career.

The weather had been warm for September in London, but nothing could have prepared Milton for the heat that swamped him when he arrived in Dubai. It was as if he had walked into the firing line of a blowtorch. Despite it being 1.00 a.m., it was hot, very hot. Bloody hot!

He battled through the huge crowds of Asians and Africans hanging around the arrivals lounge and saw the welcoming sign of his name written on a placard held by a smartly dressed Indian man.

"Hi, I am Mr Milton," he said, shaking hands and dabbing his leaking brow with a small handkerchief.

"Welcome to Dubai, Mr Milton, where all your dreams come true."

If only life were that simple, Milton thought. But he was happy to have arrived and didn't want to dampen the spirits of his jolly new companion.

"My name is Gopal and I will be driving you to your hotel, which is about 15 minutes from here. Let me take your bags, sir."

The slightly built young man, who was only around five feet tall, reached for Milton's larger-than-average suitcase and could barely lift it from the floor. Milton grabbed it back from him and swapped it for his easier-to-handle shoulder bag.

"Why thank you, sir," said a relieved Gopal.

The pair pushed past the masses that seemed to be milling around the pavements as if waiting for the arrival of a film star.

"Oh, they are stupid some of these people," Gopal stated with a slow wobble of his head.

"They have family coming to stay and they just come and hang around the airport for the whole day. Most of them are Pakistanis you know."

Milton could detect the Indian/Pakistan rivalry instantly in Gopal, who added, "They are bloody useless at cricket too!"

Milton climbed into the back of a minibus, which was exclusively his.

His arrival in Dubai was a closely guarded secret between his unit and his superiors. The Dubai authorities were totally oblivious to his being there, although Waite had handed over the contact details of the elusive Captain Ali just in case.

"At least he can show you where the best mosques are, sir, should you need to pray," Waite had joked.

Milton intended to carry out the preliminary groundwork and then call in reinforcements if required. He decided that his role should simply be to gather intelligence. The actual operation to smash the mob should be carried out at one of the two remaining matches in France or Germany. He had given himself a week to find and befriend Jacks and to go from there.

"That is the Creek Golf Club, sir." Gopal pointed to an incredible piece of architecture situated on the banks of what looked like a wide river. "The clubhouse is in the shape of a sail you see."

Milton smiled as he saw Gopal continue to wobble his head as he spoke. His action reminded him of the old BBC comedy show *It Ain't Half Hot Mum* where the British jungle troops were joined by a hard-working Indian.

Catching him smiling in the rear-view mirror, the polite Indian enquired, "What is so funny?" Again he wobbled his head.

"That is!" he replied.

"What is?" he asked with another wobble.

"The fact that you wobble your head every time you speak. Why do you do it?"

"Oh, sir, it is Indian tradition. Whenever we speak we wobble our heads, just like in England you move your hands when you talk, no?"

"I suppose so," admitted Milton, moving his hands in acceptance.

"You blondies call us Jinglies here in Dubai."

"Jinglies?"

"Yes, Jinglies. You see you blondies think we wobble our heads like a bell ringing." Gopal then broke out into song: "Jinglie bells, jinglie bells, jinglie all the way ... you know the song. See? Jinglies?"

Milton nodded with a chuckle. He felt comfortable with his new companion.

"Gopal, how about you take me on a quick guided tour of the city? I'm not feeling tired at all and I will make it worth your while. I will tell your boss that I got lost at the airport or something."

"Very well, Mr Milton, I will show you Dubai by night."

On first impression, Dubai looked spectacular.

His journey from the airport took him over Maktoum Bridge, which straddled the two oldest parts of the city, Bur Dubai and Deira. The piece of water it traversed was called the Creek, an inlet on which the city was developed.

Despite it now being almost 2.00 a.m., the city seemed alive, the roads buzzing with cars and taxis and the Creek lined with small wooden boats stacked full of just about everything imaginable.

Gopal explained that the boats were called dhows and were used by Iranians, Omanis and various other nationalities from the region for transportation. He said that everything from kitchen sinks to weapons and drugs were transported, not to mention illegal immigrants.

"If you get into trouble with the police, this is your lifeline out of here on one of those!" Gopal had pointed out.

After driving through Bur Dubai, Gopal looked to be heading towards a stretch of highway lying at the foot of a huge number of high-rise buildings, which comprised of some incredible architecture.

"These are the tampax towers," laughed Gopal.

"Please explain?" asked an increasingly inquisitive Milton.

"You see, these buildings are where many of the Emirates Airline hostesses live. You just haven't lived in Dubai until you have woken up in one of these buildings!"

He went on to point out the blue building, pink building and white building. Surely Gopal did not speak from experience? Milton thought.

It was an incredible stretch of road, with maybe 30 skyscrapers and the highlight being two enormous buildings at its entrance.

"Those are the Emirates Towers, second only to Kuala Lumpur as the tallest towers in the world. It is a five-star hotel and an office block. Very nice, no?"

Milton looked up at the towers with mouth ajar. Indeed it was impressive and he had the feeling that money was no object when it came to construction in Dubai.

Gopal continued to drive down the four-lane highway, weaving in and out of traffic as if there were no rules of the road. At one stage he had to pull sharply out of the fast lane as a light yellow Ferrari flashed by in a blur with two young Arabs in national dress in the front.

"They are crazy kids and you just get the hell out of their way," shouted Gopal from the front.

"Whatever you do in Dubai, Mr Milton, just remember not to upset a local Arab because you will be in deep trouble. Just keep your distance from them and you will love it here. They are okay in general but they can have you thrown into prison with a simple phone call to a brother, cousin, or uncle in the local police force."

"Thank you, Gopal," Milton said and realised he had just absorbed some priceless information.

The tour continued into an area known as Jumeirah. Gopal explained that this was where a lot of the Arabs and richer expatriates lived. It was a huge, sprawling urban area with some of the grandest houses Milton had ever set eyes on. There were statues of eagles and horses on gates, Porsches and just about every sports car and four-wheel utility parked out front, not to mention CCTV and elaborate lighting.

"They say that the Russian mafia run their operations from Jumeirah," said Gopal, who then unsubstantiated his claim. "Although that could be me talking just rubbish."

After driving for what seemed like forever through the maze of grand housing complexes and villas, the tour arrived at Dubai's jewel in the crown.

"They say that this place cost over one billion dollars to build. Not bad for a hotel, no?"

It was the place that Milton had seen on numerous travel programmes and now there it was in all its glory, the Burj Al Arab.

"It translates as the Arabian Tower. It has 200 suites and they say the Sultan of Brunei hires a whole floor when he comes to visit."

It was an incredible sight.

Gopal parked up at the entrance and Milton climbed out to take a closer look at this awesome feat of engineering, although as there were guards on the gate it could only be admired from a distance.

Built on a man-made island some 100 yards offshore, the Burj Al Arab stood at 400 metres high, making it the tallest hotel in the world. It was erected in the shape of a sail and a dramatic light show changed the hotel's canopy from yellow to green to blue at regular intervals. Parked out front were a dozen silver Rolls Royces and flames gushed out of two pillars at the entrance.

"The Rolls Royces are for airport pick-ups. Unfortunately the Pheasant Hotel can only afford this shitty minibus."

Gopal went on to explain that real gold was used in the hotel's interior and only the best of everything went into its fixtures and fittings.

"They say it will never recoup the expenditure, but that was not the point of its construction. It has helped to put Dubai on the map, which in turn attracts people here. You see the ruling family here are very clever. They know they have to spend to attract. That is why in Britain you people are so stupid."

The comment made Milton raise his eyebrows, but he resisted the temptation to say something argumentative and just listened.

"Take your Millennium Dome, for example," Gopal continued, and Milton started to realise that he was dealing with a very bright young man.

"Biggest waste of money in our history," replied Milton.

"You see, that is where you are wrong."

Milton continued to listen with interest.

"Okay, so the Dome itself doesn't make money. But do you think people come to Britain just to look at one thing and then leave? Of course not. The Dome helps to attract people into the country who then spend money on hotels, restaurants, transport, shops, etcetera, etcetera, etcetera. If you then add together the money they spend as a total, you will see that the Dome in fact has helped to put billions of tourism pounds into the economy."

Gopal did have a point, and as they pulled away from the splendid Burj Al Arab Milton asked, "So how come you know so much about these things?"

"Oh, sir, I have a degree in tourism marketing from the University of Calcutta," he replied with huge pride.

"So why on earth are you here driving a bus to and from the airport," asked Milton, who was saddened by what he heard next.

Gopal went on to explain that almost every penny of his parents' savings had gone into his education and what little was left they had paid to an employment agent who promised riches in the Middle East for their eldest son.

Gopal had thought he was travelling to the land of milk and honey to become a marketing manager for a five-star hotel. It was only after arriving that he found out that in fact he was taking up the position of a driver at the three-star Pheasant Hotel.

Unable to tell his family for fear of breaking their hearts, he had continued the job for the past 15 months, sending all available money back to India for nine members of his family to live off.

"How much do you earn if you don't mind my asking?"

The reply shocked Milton even more.

"Six hundred dirhams per month and I work 14 hours per day for six days!"

Simple calculation told Milton that this man was getting paid just over 100 pounds per month for almost 350 hours' work.

"That is outrageous," he said. You should report them to the authorities for that sort of treatment. It is slave labour."

"Nothing I can do, Mr Milton sir." Gopal's wobbling head was prominent again. "No one would listen. There is no minimum wage and I'm afraid that there are thousands, if not millions, of people from my home country who would love to be in my position. I am just lucky to have a job. You know hotel managers don't earn this wage back home and I also get bed and food so it is not too bad."

Milton just couldn't work it out. He had seen splendour beyond his wildest dreams in the past hour and yet the people who made the place tick were being treated no better than animals. Even the dogs in the Met Police got bed and food, he thought.

This astute young man, with a college education that would make him a relatively wealthy man in the West, was earning little more than the animals in his own police force.

It angered Milton, but the smiling face of his driver and his pleasant nature told him that he was a happy man and he had no reason to get involved. After all, he was there to do a job and get out as soon as possible.

"Here we are, Mr Milton sir, the Pheasant Hotel. I am sorry it is not quite the Burj Al Arab but it is clean and tidy nonetheless," said Gopal.

Milton peeled a 50 dirham note - worth less than 10 pounds - from his wad and slipped it into Gopal's top pocket. It was the equivalent of half a week's wages for the young man, who accepted it with glee.

"Thanks a million, my friend," Milton said with a slight wobble of his head. In response Gopal laughed and hugged Milton with great affection.

Milton knew he may need someone with Gopal's local street sense and made sure he got his mobile phone number during the journey back.

Indeed the Pheasant Hotel was not quite the Burj Al Arab, but Milton was feeling tired now and was desperate to catch some sleep. He had a long day ahead of him tomorrow and was eager to wake up fresh. He checked in and got to his room quickly. He was so tired that he could not actually remember going to bed.

Chapter 8

The howl from a mosque brought an earth-shattering halt to Milton's sleep.

Such was the volume of the rant that Milton thought someone had broken into his hotel room and placed a megaphone next to his ear. It gave him an almighty shock.

He sat upright in his bed and looked at his clock, which revealed it was still only 4.30 a.m.! He slouched back on the bed and placed a cushion over his head.

He promised himself that the first thing he would do that morning would be to buy earplugs, as the drone of the air conditioning unit ensured there was no let up between the melodic efforts.

He had noticed on his way in that the mosque was quite a way from the hotel, but had failed to notice that it had hired Ozzy Osbourne's sound system. Dubai, Milton concluded, would take some getting used to.

He wondered how Muslims must feel in the UK on a Sunday morning when the church bells are ringing out at the crack of dawn. The local vicar would probably be forced to stop or ring them later in the day by some whacky local council.

But then again, he thought, he was in someone else's country after all and, despite Britain deciding it would bend over backwards to allow people to do whatever they wanted, there was no reason why other countries should.

When in Rome do as the Romans do, he thought. Or, more appropriately, when in Arabia, do as the Arabs do. He decided he would just accept the culture rather than become a part of it.

If only people would do that when arriving in England, he pondered. Then there would be a more harmonious melting pot of religions and nationalities rather than the splintered mess it had become.

Milton eventually needed his alarm call from the young female voice on the other end of the phone to wake him at 10.00 a.m. It was pushing 6.00 a.m. before he had finally got back to sleep so he had enjoyed four uninterrupted hours. He was sure he would have been there until the next mullah's offering had the phone not rang.

It was Sunday morning. Milton looked through his curtains into the bright sunshine and was shocked to see the roads outside alive with traffic. It was, after all, a working day in Dubai with Friday being the holy day of rest in the Middle East, as a frustrated Sergeant Waite had discovered two days earlier.

There were cars, bikes, buses and lorries jostling for the best positions on the roads and honking their horns at nothing in particular. The Pheasant Hotel wasn't exactly sitting in the quietest part of town or overlooking a bronze beach, but at least it was centrally located. The chaotic traffic outside told him that.

There was a thud at the door, and an Asian-sounding "Room Service" followed as a young waiter steered the trolley through the narrow entrance to the centre of Milton's decent-sized abode.

"Eggs on toast, sir, and the top English paper here, the *Gulf News*, as ordered," said the smart waiter, who shared the same head-wobbling foible as Gopal had displayed the previous evening.

Milton gave the boy a couple of crisp notes and tucked into his first square meal for some time. His last day had been a rush and food had been only an afterthought. Airline food was airline food - it filled a small hole, but eggs on toast - the single man's banquet - was what he really needed now.

The index on the front of the *Gulf News* indicated that the UK news was on page 11, so he flicked directly past the opening pages.

Despite it now being almost two weeks since the match in Switzerland, even papers as far away as Dubai hadn't forgotten those disgraceful scenes.

'Police arrest hooligans following paper's appeal' said the page lead.

The story described how *The Sun* had published pictures of the troublemakers and asked people to ring the hooligan hotline to reveal their identities. In doing so, those people were awarded 100 pounds.

The Sun's patriotic editor was quoted as saying: "We know how important it is to stop this mindless football violence. We want the World Cup in England in 2006 and we will do our bit to blitz Fritz and ensure that happens."

Milton appreciated help from any quarter, but knew he was on the strongest trail yet and the media back home hadn't got a whiff of it.

Milton made a call back to the UK but had forgotten that London was three hours behind and so caught Waite in bed at 7.10 a.m. on a Sunday morning. Well, he had gained revenge on Waite for the previous Sunday when he had enjoyed a few pints down the local himself.

"Glad to know the mice aren't at play while the cat's away," Milton said sarcastically before hanging up. Revenge was sweet.

He was still feeling exhausted and was in no mood for trawling through the streets of a new city. He had picked up plenty of literature from the hotel's amply stocked information booth and had purchased a couple of magazine guides from the shop in the lobby.

He also knew that if he were to fit in he needed to look as though he had been in Dubai for some time, so he retired to the hotel's rooftop swimming pool to do some reading.

As the sun belted down, Milton became engrossed in how Dubai had become the city it was today.

For centuries, the Arabs of Dubai had been dependent on the seas. Fishing and pearl diving were their two main lifelines, but the discovery of oil in the 1950s changed everything. Its people moved from shanty Bedouin villages to plush properties supplied by the Government and the Europeans moved in as the promise of tax-free riches brought Western expertise to the desert.

Road systems and bridges led the structural revolution that was to launch Dubai into a modern-day city. Buildings followed and, as the ruling family realised the country couldn't survive on oil forever, so came business and tourism.

As a result, Dubai soon became the leisure, tourism and business hub of the Middle East and the crossroads between East and West, North and South.

Its current population was estimated to be over one million, with around 100,000 of those coming from the West. Most of these were of course young and single professionals, and where there are young and single people, nightlife must flourish.

Dubai had managed to create a vibrant night scene and one guide to a night out said it was home to 1,000 pubs and over 50 nightclubs. The majority of those were located in hotels across the city.

As Milton delved deeper into the almanacs of Dubai, he realised that he was reading about one of the world's best kept secrets and couldn't wait to get out there and discover it for himself.

A flick through the local yellow pages, or blue pages just to be different, gave him the phone number of Expatriatedotcom and his undercover work would start early the very next morning.

First though, he thought to himself as he smothered more sun oil on his chest, he must discover whether Dubai really was the place that the brochures and magazines had promised. But that could wait, so he pushed his sunbed backrest parallel to the floor and lay back under the clear blue sky.

It was now 9.00 p.m. and the guest liaison manager told Milton of a few watering holes that would be popular choice to visit on a Sunday night.

Milton wanted a feel for the nightlife, as he thought it could be helpful later on. Nothing would be worse than if he managed to infiltrate Jacks and his men only for one to ask, "So where do you do your drinking?"

He had to know Dubai like a regular, and while he felt he had a good grasp of the tourist daytime routes, thanks to the pamphlets, he must scratch beneath the surface to discover the nightlife.

"So what exactly are you looking for?" asked the guest liaison manager.

"Well, somewhere lively. Somewhere to get a beer and ..." He was almost embarrassed to say.

"Somewhere for women?" finished the smiling man who was sitting behind a desk covered in pamphlets.

"Yes, that's right, somewhere where the ladies go," added a more confident Milton.

The manager jumped up from behind his desk and signalled the valet parker over. In turn he led Milton to the door, flagged down a taxi and uttered some instruction, which was probably in Hindi, to the driver.

Milton had been in Dubai for a whole day and had hardly seen an Arab. Indians and Pakistanis were everywhere and it underscored the theory that Gopal had shared with him the night before: that Dubai was kept ticking by expat labour.

"Why don't I see any of the Arabs working?" enquired Milton to the bearded taxi driver, who looked like an Afghan or Iranian.

"They take the jobs in banks and government ministries. It is left to us to do all the hard work," was the reply. "Sometimes, sir, your path in life depends solely on the place of your birth. I sometimes wonder if God meant it that way or whether somewhere along the line he has simply turned his back on humans to let us just get on with it."

As the car weaved through the busy traffic, Milton could tell from the driver's accent that he was another well-educated man who, like Gopal, had probably been duped into working in the Middle East by some rogue employment agent operating on the subcontinent.

After no more than ten minutes, Milton was dropped off at a white building which was covered in bright orange lighting in what looked like a whirlwind blowing up and down its wall.

"This is the Cyclone Club, sir. You will find everything you are looking for in there," said the taxi driver as Milton uneasily edged himself out of the car.

He paid the driver and walked towards two burly white doormen who asked for his membership card in what sounded like Russian-English. When Milton replied that he was a tourist the men let him through and ordered him to pay the equivalent of five pounds to a petite Filipino woman behind a till.

He could hear loud music inside and walked through a thick swing door to be confronted by a sight that could have been anywhere in the Western world.

It was only 10.00 p.m., but Milton had walked into a scene from *The Rocky Horror Picture Show*.

Dance music was pumping, the dance floor was full and the bar was lined by an assortment of women that could easily have made up the United Nations.

Rubbing his hands, Milton headed towards the bar.

He wedged himself between two well-developed, top-heavy black women and called up a Budweiser from another Filipino woman behind the bar.

Before the drink returned, he felt a hand move down his back and towards his bottom.

Turning to his right, he was faced by a wide toothy smile from one of the ladies who said in broken English. "You looking for lady, handsome?"

Milton was shocked and took a step back from the bar, politely refusing.

He walked around the huge circular bar and noticed that he was being watched by literally dozens of pairs of eyes. He felt like a hunter in a forest, with his prey watching his every move from the relative safety of the scrub, only here it seemed as if the prey was doing anything it could to be caught.

As he stood by the corner of the dance floor to take it all in, another beauty took him by surprise.

"I could love you long time tonight, mister."

This time the girl was lighter skinned and was caressing the back of his hair in circular motions with her index finger.

She was a cracker and Milton, accepting he was no Mel Gibson, knew something had to be up. He had either stumbled across 'Milton World' where every woman was in love with him or, which seemed more probable, the Cyclone Club was a hooker bar.

"So what do you do here in Dubai?" asked Milton.

"I am business lady," she replied in easy-to-understand English.

"What sort of business?"

"Whatever you like. Two hundred dollar and I give you good business all night."

She finished her sentence with a girly laugh.

Milton had found a part of Dubai that had certainly not made its way into the tourist guides but, judging by the number of people there, it was a thriving side of the city.

"I will give you ten dollars if you spend five minutes chatting to me, and I'll even throw in a drink," said Milton.

She agreed and walked with Milton to a quiet corner of the club where he would not have to shout over the music.

The prostitute told Milton that she had been working in Dubai for two years and was looked after by a local man. He ensured that the authorities turned a blind eye to her activities in return for a share of her profits and free sex. She said the local man looked after 30 girls who worked a number of bars across the city.

She had escaped war in Eritrea with her sister and lived in a one-bedroom flat with three other girls. She was earning a good living. Dubai has a major port and there were no shortage of sailors and servicemen willing to pay for her services. Not to mention unsuspecting businessmen and, of course, the expatriates living in the city - generally the married ones too, she had added.

"I sometimes make up to two thousand dollar a month," she said.

Milton was shocked. He presumed that many a businessman looking for a club for beer and ladies must end up there. The only way the wife would ever find out is if they returned home with the sort of gift that would require a joint visit to the local clap clinic.

The information was an eye-opener once again and, looking around the club, he exclaimed to the girl, "I just cannot believe I am sitting in the Middle East!"

There was only one word to describe it ... seedy!

He was surrounded by men groping women, women groping men and, in one case, a woman groping a woman. There was dancing on tables, in fact dancing anywhere a space could be found, and the beer seemed to be flowing in huge amounts.

He decided, though, that this was more a place for visitors and that he needed to tap into the social route taken by Dubai's residents.

He finished the last of his Budweiser with two gulps, slipped the prostitute the money he promised and headed towards the exit. She had told him of a few other places to try that were 'hooker-free', as she put it.

He had ended up spending an hour talking to the girl, but the night was still young. He had read that everywhere in Dubai was open until 3.00 a.m. every night of the week, so there were still five hours of adventuring to be done.

The now familiar site of an Asian-driven taxi took him to another splendid hotel and the smartly dressed doorman took one look at him and informed him that the 'Old Vic' was located on the third floor.

As the name suggests, the Old Vic was a typically English pub and it was full of British expatriates playing darts, pool or just having a pint.

This is more like it, Milton thought. He didn't want to start asking questions just yet; that could wait until the following day. No, tonight was for finding his feet and he felt he was doing well so far.

His tour took him to three more bars frequented by British drinkers and he made notes of each one to keep them fresh in his mind.

Now if he was asked, "So where do you do your drinking?" he could reel off a list of four pubs and finish off by saying, "And if I'm desperate I'll pop down for a last dance at the Cyclone!"

It was almost 2.30 a.m. by the time he arrived back at the Pheasant Hotel. The same valet driver was standing by the hotel entrance and seemed surprised when Milton climbed out of the taxi alone.

"You not like the lady?" he enquired.

"No, lady fine," he replied, brushing past him and heading through the lobby semi-drunk.

"Lady very fine, just John not too fine, very sleepy," Milton found himself replying in broken English too as he pointed to himself.

He had enjoyed a fruitful first day. He may even have seen Jacks in one of those pubs, although he had studied the picture on the driving licence well and, even though it was black and white, he was confident he would recognise Jacks if he saw him in the flesh.

The serious surveillance work must begin the next day and he had secured the services of the one man in Dubai he could rely on the most.

Chapter 9

As promised, Gopal was parked just around the corner of the Pheasant Hotel waiting for Milton at 11.00 a.m.

The young Indian didn't want to be seen by his bosses so close to his workplace on his day off. They suspected that members of staff were acting as guides on their days off and instant dismissal and a plane straight back to India would be the consequence.

Gopal was behind the wheel of a fairly sturdy pick-up.

"Good morning, sir," he said with a chauffeur-like smile and salute as Milton climbed into the passenger seat.

"This is a nice motor, Gopal. How can you manage to afford something like this?" asked Milton.

"Ah, sir, this is part of the Gopal Empire. I bought this pick-up with four friends. We each have a different day off in the week and on those days we drive around the city and offer to help pull people out of the sand. Once I pulled a Porsche out of the sand and the man gave me 500 dirhams. That is almost my month's salary with the hotel!"

Milton had already got used to Gopal's head wobbling. If he had not it would have driven him insane!

"Very industrious, Gopal, very industrious indeed," he replied.

"This way, sir, my family thinks I am earning big bucks in the hotel in management. If they knew what I was really doing they would be heartbroken."

Milton admired Gopal and they chatted on their way to the stake-out located on an industrial estate just two miles out of the city.

Milton's adrenalin was starting to pump in the same way it did at the start of most stake-outs. He had packed a digital camera with a strong zoom lens so they could keep a safe distance from their targets. A good job too, as the pick-up hardly offered much in the form of camouflage.

Gopal knew his way around the city and had done his homework the night before to ensure that they could drive straight to the warehouse of

Exptriatedotcom that morning.

He parked on the side of the road a safe distance from the warehouse and turned off the engine. It was now around 11.30 a.m. and the day was starting to heat up.

"What do we do now, sir?" asked Gopal.

"Well, Gopal my friend, we just sit, wait and observe. Do you think we can turn on the air conditioning?" said Milton.

"Oh sir, no sir," replied Gopal.

"Why not?" enquired Milton.

"Well, sir, we don't actually have it fitted in this vehicle. Couldn't afford it, so we just drive around with the window open."

Not wanting to show his annoyance, Milton wound down the window, but this offered little comfort as it was now starting to get just as hot outside.

It was a huge warehouse and the Expatriatedotcom logo was in full view above what looked like the main entrance. In the car park at the front was an assortment of shiny sports cars and four-wheel drives. An interesting first impression. In fact there wasn't a Ford Escort or a Honda Civic in sight.

Milton remembered back to Captain Ali's information, which stated that Jacks was the head of this company and it employed some 50 English nationals. He looked at the car park and concluded that business must be booming for Expatriatedotcom. After all, how many warehouses and factories back in the UK would boast a car park rivalling that of a Premier League football team?

He had asked Waite to check out the company on the Internet the previous day and email through any pages of importance.

As Captain Ali had said, the company supplied patriotic merchandise to people and companies across the world of all nationalities and claimed to be the biggest online global distributor of national flags.

Milton was reading the pages that Waite had emailed through to him and one particular section he found interesting came under 'jobs'.

It stated: "We are looking for ex-servicemen proud to be English and not afraid of hard work and who would enjoy working with a great bunch of like-minded lads. Age 30-40 and partial to travel. An interest in football is beneficial though not essential."

Why on earth would a company want to add that to a recruitment advert? This particular part, Milton and his racing mind concluded, linked Jacks and the men with whom he hired the helicopter to the man on the ground caught on that snippet of CCTV film fighting like Bruce Lee in Zurich.

It was as if Jacks was assembling his own British army right here in the Middle East. The plot thickens, Milton thought. Although his thick plots had sunk all too often on this case in the past.

After about 30 minutes, Gopal was visibly bored so Milton told him he could go and hang out at a nearby roadside café, allowing Milton to mull over his theories and thoughts in relative peace and quiet.

For the next couple of hours, Milton roasted in the cab of the pick-up but managed to get four or five snaps of men pulling up and entering the building. Most were athletic looking with closely cropped hair and carrying sports bags.

Are these men going to work or going to play football? Milton thought to himself as he flicked through the digital images on his camera's LCD screen.

Gopal returned to the pick-up with some food. Not doughnuts, as Milton was hoping for, but some spicy Indian dips. Milton was hungry through boredom by now and gleefully accepted.

"How's it going, sir?" enquired Gopal.

"Not bad but a little slow. You need patience in this game, Gopal my friend, you can't force the issue," he explained.

"Like test match cricket you mean?" said Gopal. "You English love your test match cricket but we love the one-day matches. I mean, what is the point in playing for five days and sometimes not even getting a result?"

Milton was amused by the comparison and entered into a deep conversation about cricket - a game he did know something about - and good old English traditions.

For a moment they managed to escape their current predicament, but not for long. Their conversation comparing fish and chips to curry was interrupted by the revving of a powerful car engine, which was coming from the other side a chin-high wall behind them.

Milton jumped from his seat and tiptoed to see over the wall. On the other side was a black Range Rover with its rear right wheel deep in sand and sinking deeper with each roar of the engine.

Milton could see the driver was European and, as he moved to look from the back, he noticed the red and white of a St George's flag sticker on the back, close to the boot handle.

This could be his chance. Although he had originally planned to infiltrate through a chance meeting in a pub or a shop, he knew that whoever was driving this motor probably worked at Expatriatedotcom, which was less than 50 yards away from where the Range Rover was stuck.

He walked around the wall and jogged over to the driver who had just hung up on his mobile phone.

"Look's like you're stuck deep," said Milton.

"These bloody Range Rovers are hopeless," said the driver in a broad Cockney accent. "Third time this has happened to me in a week."

"Can I give you a tow?" Milton offered while inspecting the problem.

"Thanks, mate, but I've just called one of the lads at work and he said he would come over."

Milton was slightly annoyed but …

"On the other hand, mate, knowing Chalky it will take him an hour to get here so a tow would be the dogs nuts."

Milton scurried back to the pick-up where Gopal was waiting. He told him to make himself scarce and drove around to the front of the Range Rover.

"Pain in the arse this, mate," said the Cockney. "I only bought this a month ago and haven't quite got used to it. I'll have to stop taking the short cut to work and keep to the roads."

Milton could see this was close to a brand spanking new motor, one that even his boss would struggle to afford back home.

The pair chained up the Range Rover's bumper to the back of the pick-up and after a couple of tries the vehicle wriggled free of its sand trap and onto harder ground.

Milton jumped out of the pick-up and jogged back to the Range Rover behind to retrieve the tow rope.

"Hey, thanks mate." The Cockney went to the back of the vehicle and offered his hand in friendship.

"No problems. It was the least I could do."

"Alvin Insdale," he introduced himself. "But my mates call me Stardust after the singer."

Milton frowned, not making the link.

"Alvin Stardust? '70s? Dodgy hair?" Stardust gave his clues. "Oh, never mind. I'd never heard of him neither til I came here!"

Milton nodded in acknowledgement and introduced himself. "John Milton, but my mates call me Milton, after my surname!"

They shook hands, but Milton realised that he had just revealed his true identity. However, he was pretty much an anonymous figure with the force and was confident he could at least retain his name during this operation.

"So what do you do in Dubai, Milton?" asked Stardust.

"Well, to be honest," Milton stumbled as he realised he hadn't even cooked up a proper tale yet, "I'm actually looking for work."

"Really, what is it you do?"

Remembering the information on the jobs page on the Internet, he replied, "To be honest, I'm not qualified in too much. You see I left the army only a couple of years back because my wife hated me being away and as it turned out she left me anyway!"

"Bitch, mate, but I see you still wear the ring."

Big mistake number one - the wedding band was still on his hand. Milton knew he had to sharpen up his act.

"Well, you know, nostalgia."

Milton went on to tell Stardust that he had been working as a security guard since arriving back on civvie street and just wanted to get as far away from his ruined domestic life as possible. This was actually not far off the truth.

"Me and the missus came out here on holiday last year and I loved it so much that I decided to come back for a few weeks to give it a bash, but I'm running out of time and money."

"Well Milton, this could be your lucky day," said Stardust. "The company I work for is always on the lookout for the likes of you and I'll have a word with the boss to see what he thinks. What's your mobile number?"

"I'm sorry I don't have one."

There was a brief pause as Stardust worked out how he could assist his helper.

"Well, never mind, just make it to the Carter's bar in the Pyramids complex tomorrow night at 9.00 p.m. when we all get together from work. I'll introduce you to the guv'nor and we'll go from there."

With that, another four-wheel drive motor came roaring through the sand and did a handbrake turn to finish up in front of the pick-up.

"Someone call for the RAC?" said the light brown skinned man in what sounded like an East Anglian accent.

"Jesus Christ, Chalky. I would've died of starvation if I'd waited for you. Chalky, this is John Milton, my knight in shining armour. Milton, this is Chalky, an absolute plonker."

The three laughed and returned to their vehicles. As Milton tied up the tow rope in the cab, he knew he had made his breakthrough. Stardust had unwittingly unlocked the door to welcome the enemy and, come tomorrow night, Milton was determined that not only would he have infiltrated Jacks and his merry men, but also he would have got a job in the heart of the operation he was trying to smash.

"Now that is how to do surveillance work," he muttered as he turned the key in the ignition and pressed the accelerator towards the floor.

The pick-up did not move and he knew he had just got himself stuck in the sand. It took him and Gopal over two hours in the burning early afternoon sun to dig it out, but at least it topped up his tan.

Chapter 10

Gopal was unable to provide Milton with much information on the Carter's Bar or the Pyramids complex.

"They don't like Asians like me going in there much," he had said on the way back to the Pheasant Hotel. "It is very nice and they only like the rich Asians, Europeans and Arabs going in there."

Stardust had told him to be there at 9.00 p.m., but Milton didn't want to seem too keen and arrived at the bar an hour later. It was indeed an incredible building. The brochure he had read the day before informed him that it was one of the city's leading entertainment complexes with a number of restaurants and bars.

Carter's was located at the top of a marble staircase and a burly doorman saw his white face and waved him past a small queue of Asian couples.

He felt guilty as he edged past the couple at the front and into one of the most elegant bars he had ever seen. The high roof had colonial-style fans blowing cool air onto the revelling masses below.

The bar sprawled the entire length of the club to his left, so he edged past a couple of chatting English girls and ordered a beer. He overheard the girls talking about their schedules and jumped easily to the conclusion that they were air hostesses.

He turned away from the bar, leaned back on his elbows, and saw that the club was packed with beautiful European-looking women and an equal splattering of blokes.

It looked like a free-for-all and the alcohol was flowing like a river.

It could have been Ibiza in the height of summer.

The place was electric, but he knew tonight was probably the most important night of his career. He had to infiltrate and this was his big chance. Cock up tonight and he could probably kiss goodbye to any chance of finding out the real story of Carson Jacks. With it he could probably kiss goodbye to his career.

His head rotated around the club like that of an owl on its perch and he soon noticed a mob of seven well-dressed thirty-somethings sitting on sofas and easy chairs in the far corner of the club.

They laughed loudly and looked like a typical bunch of British lads enjoying a Saturday night on the town, only this was a school night. It was Tuesday.

Milton monitored them for a short while and noticed both Stardust and Chalky. He was in business.

The table was covered in empty beer bottles and a number of smaller glasses that showed they had also consumed their fair share of shooters.

Then Milton, who was standing in the crowd about ten yards away from them, was pushed out of the way by a waiter who was carrying a tray of flaming drinks at shoulder height and making his way towards the table. His arrival at the table was met by cheers of approval from the gang who swiftly grabbed a glass each.

Stardust declared, "One for all and all for one."

The flaming beverages disappeared as quick as they had arrived and the cheers continued as the glasses slammed down in unison on the table in front of them.

Milton knew he had to make his move.

He walked up the two steps towards the men and was spotted immediately. "Here he is, fellas, the one and only John Milton," heralded Stardust.

This was met by a ranting chorus that made him feel as though he had gatecrashed a stag night. "He is the meanest, he sucks the horse's penis, John Milton is the horse's arse!"

Milton felt he had already made new friends.

"Come and meet the lads, Milton." Stardust put his arm around Milton's shoulder and led him into the lion's den.

Stardust rattled off a load of nicknames and Milton tried to remember as many as possible but it was like listening to road directions. He remembered the first couple and just nodded as the others were announced.

However, then he was told a name that he had heard plenty of times over the last couple of weeks.

"Hi Milton, I'm Carson Jacks, nice to meet you. Take a seat. Come and join us."

Milton was almost star-struck as he took a seat. He had built up a hatred for this man over the previous couple of weeks and yet it was one of the warmest introductions he had ever experienced.

Jacks resembled his black and white photo on the driving licence but, if the truth be known, he was a hell of a good-looking bloke. He was just under six feet tall with dark, spiky, ruffled hair. It was the sort of style that Milton saw on the wall of his local barber's shop, telling punters that they too could look like the model in the picture for just 100 quid.

Although the club was dark, there was enough light to see that Jacks had dark brown eyes. He had a square jawline chiselled with dominant cheekbones. Milton guessed he was about 12 to 13 stone with an athletic build.

To be honest, there was only one word to describe the way Jacks looked, or maybe there were two: Perfect. Bastard.

"Stardust tells me you came to his rescue yesterday," said Jacks. "You should have just left him in the sand considering how much work he did when he got there."

A roar of laughter from the other guys met the comment. Stardust's response was a middle finger flicked in the general direction of them all.

"Well, I don't like to see anyone in trouble. Military training taught me that," said Milton, unleashing his fairy tale.

"Who did you serve with?" asked Jacks.

"The Grenadier Guards."

"Interesting. How long were you in for?"

"Almost eight years, until the wife decided enough was enough." Milton had tightened up his story that day and researched plenty of information on the Grenadier Guards to make it watertight.

"Yeah, sorry to hear about the wife. Stardust told me about that too. Any tours of duty?"

"Well, the usual, Northern Ireland twice, Germany for three years and the odd field trip to Belize and Cyprus. Nothing too exciting really."

Milton could not work out if he was being interviewed or interrogated. Whichever, he knew he had to be on his toes. His interviewer-cum-interrogator may have drunk plenty of booze but he was still in complete control. He spoke well and was a smooth operator.

"Well, it is all in the past now, my friend," said Jacks as he drew Milton's attention to the swathe of pale-skinned beauties adorning the bar. "Here in Desert England it is all about now and the future. No time to wallow in the past!"

"Desert England?" enquired Milton.

"Yes, Desert England. Look around you. You will see more English people in the bars and nightclubs here than you will in any city back home. Tens of thousands of us here," said Jacks. "And as you may have noticed, we are in the middle of a desert. Hence, Dubai is known to us expats as Desert England."

Milton acknowledged the clarification and figured it would not be long before some travel company picked up on this excellent marketing slogan.

"Stardust tells me you are looking for a job? Consider tonight as your induction to Expatriatedotcom. If you survive it, we will see what we can do. If you do not, just give us your dog tags and we will make sure your immediate family are informed," Jacks said in a serious voice as the rest of the guys sat and stared with poker faces as though their chief meant it. Milton felt a sudden sense of uneasiness.

But it did not take long for Jacks's straight face to break into a smile and a laugh, which sparked off another drunken chorus. This must have been a stag night.

Milton spent the next hour drinking a mixture of flaming concoctions and exotic beers imported from countries he never even knew existed. More importantly, he was getting to know the man who could hold the key to this whole operation, Carson Jacks.

He was class. He did not give away anything about himself but managed to extract plenty of information from Milton. He was getting to know his potential new recruit.

Each time Milton asked about Expatriatedotcom, Jacks simply replied that he would learn plenty if he got through the night, and, to Milton's dismay, the next day.

"Your induction does not just finish tonight, Milton. Wait until tomorrow!" said Chalky with a wink from across the table.

Milton felt that he was sitting with a film star. Everyone in the bar seemed to know Jacks. Girls were flirting as they walked past and tried to catch eye contact. The lads outside his powerful inner circle were all pretending - or wishing - to be his friend.

Milton deduced that this was a man he would have looked up to and admired in his younger days: surrounded by friends, captain of the football team, never without a girl and always one in reserve. Carson Jacks would never have suffered from acne. School work would not have been a problem. For sure, his mother would never have caught him in his room, trousers down, with a third-hand copy of *Razzle*.

There was no clear accent, maybe southern although chipped away at over the years to create a clear, unique tone.

The guy was simply class.

Not surprisingly, Milton was now starting to feel fairly drunk and he was proving a hit with his new 'friends'. He was actually enjoying his night and felt accepted. They all seemed a good bunch.

There was Kirk. Apparently he gained his nickname from Captain Kirk.

"This man will go to places that no other man will go," said Stardust during their introduction. "Whether the woman is green, blue, has two heads or three eyes; Kirk will crack it. The man has no morals or standards! He is a 24-carat dirty sod!"

Chalky was called Chalky, not because of some tired old slant towards his brown skin, but simply because his name was Simon Chalk.

Then there was Lenny, who achieved his nickname due to his reputation as being the group's hard nut.

"He is bloody tough," said Stardust. Indeed, Lenny was a brute of a man but again friendly enough. A kind of gentle giant, in the same way as the man he got his nickname from, Lenny McLean the notorious London hard man of the seventies, eighties and nineties.

JT was called JT because his name was John Thomas. The lads had decided it was cruel enough being called John Thomas and so did not warrant a nickname.

Finally there was Pups. He was only 22 and the puppy of the group by some margin. He had a baby face, which made him look even younger.

Milton quickly established that while the group's favourite pastime was taking the piss out of each other, Pups, as the most junior, was at the butt end of a majority of the jokes.

"Pups struggles to get into most of the places around here because he looks too young, but that is no excuse for him being a virgin too," said Stardust, who appeared to be the main comedian.

"He is in our YTS scheme, aren't you Pups?" He looked at the youngster who nodded while at the same waiting for the expected punchline. "Young Tosser on Speed!"

Again roars of alcohol-induced laughter met the joke and Pups accepted it once again by shaking his head and joining in the laughs. Not as loud as the others though.

Milton had not enjoyed a night like this since his pre-marital years.

"Right lads, finish your shandies, it is time to move to the Planetarium," announced Jacks as they gulped down what was left of the liquor and rose in unison from their chairs. The crowd appeared to part to let Moses and his followers through to the exit.

Milton could see that that Jacks commanded respect in this town and was very much the guv'nor of the manor.

The group walked down the stairs, out of the complex and into the warm night air. They arched a left and walked for another 50 yards or so to a doorway guarded by three burley black bouncers.

"Evening lads," said one in a deep English accent.

The group filed through one by one, but Milton was stopped by a chunky hand on his shoulder from one of the men.

"Sorry, mate, you can't come in here in those. No jeans allowed on a Tuesday night. Come back tomorrow."

"Shit," Milton thought.

Jacks, who had already walked through, returned to the door.

"It's all right Tyson, he's with me," he said to the man mountain.

"Sorry, Mr Jacks. Management says we have to be strict on a Tuesday because we've been squeezing too many in," the bouncer said to Jacks apologetically.

"I understand." Jacks placed a reassuring hand on the bouncer's shoulder, which was met by a sigh of relief from the suited doorman who towered over him.

Another sign that showed Milton that Jacks was well respected. Even the doormen were wary of him.

Jacks led his group away from the door and towards the car park. As soon as they were out of sight from the bouncers he told them to huddle around him.

"Here's what we'll do," he said. "We'll all go in and Milton you wait by that window there."

He pointed to a small rectangular window with misty glass about seven feet from the ground. It was slightly open.

"That's the window for the toilets. When we go in we'll tell the blokes on the door that you have popped home to get a pair of trousers.

"Pups, you go straight to the toilet. Take off your trousers and hand them to Milton through the window. Wait in the bogs until Milton comes in to give you them back. John, you just slip them on over your jeans.

"Once inside, no one can tell if you're wearing trousers or a g-string. You okay with that, Pups? Milton?"

Both of them nodded and the huddle broke. It was as if they were approaching the final seconds of a basketball match and Jacks's team was planning its last raid. Half the team, though, was giggling as Jacks's alcohol-induced plan was unveiled.

Milton walked to the window and the group headed back to the entrance.

Milton could vaguely make out the doormen accepting Jacks's story.

"He only lives around the corner and should be back soon in trousers," he told them.

Milton leaned against the wall under the toilet window, still out of view of the bouncers.

During his five-minute wait he saw some of the most beautiful women he had ever set eyes on walk past. Some were wearing next to nothing and he knew he had to get inside that club.

Whether it was the alcohol or the buzz he was getting from mixing with his intended targets, Maggie and the kids seemed a long way away at that moment. And not just in terms of miles either.

"Milton, are you there?"

He could see Pups struggle to find him through the open window. From the commotion, Pups was either on someone's shoulders or being lifted up.

"Yeah, I'm here Pups," he whispered in reply.

"Okay, here are my trousers. Don't be long 'cause I've only got very brief briefs on, if you know what I mean. I'll wait in the last cubicle on the right. The furthest from the door."

Pups disappeared and Milton started to put the trousers on over his jeans. As he buttoned them up he heard someone rush towards him.

Jacks appeared with Lenny, JT, Kirk, Chalky and Stardust.

"Come on, let's go," Jacks said to Milton.

"But what about Pups?" asked a concerned Milton.

"Let's just say it's part of his growing-up process," said Stardust as the group headed towards the taxi rank, howls of laughter left in their wake.

As the two taxis pulled off, all Milton could think about was poor Pups, stranded in a cubicle in just his pants and shirt and waiting for his trousers to be returned.

With each time the toilet door opened, he could imagine Pups enquiring, "Milton, is that you?"

For sure, anyone that entered the toilet would think Pups was waiting for a gay friend to join him in the cubicle.

The whole scenario made Milton worry for Pups. But boy was it funny!

Pups was forgotten by the time the two-car convoy reached another city centre hotel. Just to the left of the entrance was a doorway flanked by two showpiece Harleys.

"Where are we going now?" Milton asked Stardust.

"The best club in the world, my friend, the Rock Bottom Café," interrupted JT, finishing the sentence with a poor imitation of an American accent.

The seven men entered and were met by another bouncing club with what sounded like live rock music being blasted from the stage situated just out of view to the left.

The place was packed and Milton noticed that everyone seemed to be walking around with pints of green liquid. It looked like some sort of acid.

"Welcome to the Rock Bottom Café, Milton, the home of the Bullfrog," said Jacks, who pointed to the drink that had commanded Milton's attention.

The men walked through the crowds and into a slightly smaller back room housing six pool tables. The area was not as busy and there were seven pints of the green stuff known as Bullfrogs on the bar already. Apparently one of the lads had placed the order on their mobile phone from the taxi en route.

Milton could see the men tuck into their drinks and decided to give it a go.

He took a big gulp and was pleasantly surprised.

"That ..." he said pointing to the pint, "... is very good."

"Four white spirits topped up with Red Bull. We see it as God's own concoction, sent from the heavens to make us happy," JT roared as the men gulped down the best part of the pint in one.

Kirk, who had spent the night surveying the abundance of talent, announced, "Are you guys going to stand around here playing with each other all night or are we going to find some women?"

He led the way out of the pool room and into the main area where the band was playing on a slightly raised stage.

It was a full five-piece rock band playing classics and the crowd were jumping around like kangaroos on springs.

"That's what Bullfrog does for you, mate," said Jacks to a shocked Milton.

Lenny and JT finished their drinks and jumped into the bouncing masses as Milton stayed close to Jacks, Kirk, Chalky and Stardust on the side of the 'dance floor'.

"This city is alive seven nights of the week," Jacks shouted in Milton's ear over the noise of the band's rendition of 'Should I Stay or Should I Go?' by The Clash.

"It's a young man's town and even if you're not so young, like us, it sure makes you feel young which is just as important. This place has everything: sunshine, money, women, beaches and, most importantly, Bullfrogs."

Another tray of the green stuff arrived.

As the night progressed into a green haze, the mob dispersed. At one point he did bump into Pups, who saw the funny side of the practical joke. He said they always picked on him but he was game for a laugh anyway. He had managed to buy a pair of trousers from someone in the toilet for the equivalent of 100 quid.

"I'm sure they're only worth a bloody tenner," he had said.

The last time he saw Lenny and JT they were pogoing to some Sex Pistols number and he remembered seeing Kirk living up to his reputation by walking arm in arm with a larger-than-life woman heading towards the exit.

As for Chalky, Stardust and Jacks, they seemed to just disappear at some point as people do on a piss-up. Having said that, it was now 3.00 a.m. and he had been with them half an hour earlier, so it was hardly as if they had sneaked off.

They had all gone their own drunken separate ways.

Milton staggered into the lobby of the Pheasant Hotel and the same guest liaison manager was sitting at his desk smiling.

Milton was pissed and knew he was going to regret it in the morning. He had just experienced one of the wildest nights of his life but was fearful of what tomorrow held.

Had he let anything slip during the night? He was extremely drunk but hopefully he had kept to his story.

Jacks had told him that tomorrow was part two of his induction. He was confident he had got through part one unscathed. But what was in store for him tomorrow?

Chapter 11

For the first time since arriving in Dubai, the bellow of the early morning call to prayer failed to awaken Milton from his pit.

However, something even more alarming caused him to prise his heavy eyelids apart.

"Room service," came the shout from behind the front door.

He couldn't even remember ordering room service but at that moment he wasn't even sure what universe he was in, let alone what time it was.

He struggled out of bed wearing nothing but boxer shorts and rubbed his throbbing head as he walked towards the door.

Without even looking through the peephole, he opened the door only to be jumped upon by two men. They lifted him off his feet before he could offer any resistance and barged him through the bathroom door, throwing him into the empty bath.

"Wakey, wakey, Milton, this is your morning call." Looking up through blurry eyes, he could make out Stardust and Chalky laughing hysterically as they switched on the shower, spraying water over Milton.

"How's the head, Milton?" asked Stardust.

"Damn sore," he replied, gingerly climbing to his feet.

"Sorry to surprise you, mate, but we find it's the best way to get someone up and out of bed. We'll let you get cleaned up. C'mon Chalky, you don't want to look at his bits do you?"

"Yeah right, Stardust, you're the gay boy around here," replied Chalky as he flicked Stardust's legs with a towel he had been spiralling into a lethal baton.

The pair went back into the bedroom, leaving Milton to try to get some life into his lifeless body.

He turned the shower onto the coldest setting, which still spurted out luke warm water. He had a hangover all right. One like he had not suffered for a good few years.

He slipped on a robe and walked back into the bedroom. Stardust and

Chalky were sitting on the bed watching the news.

"What time is it guys?" asked Milton.

"Just gone 9.00 a.m., cocker, and you've got five minutes to get your arse into gear and down to the lobby," said Stardust.

"You've got a long day ahead of you, mate," added Chalky.

Milton saw the pair were wearing shorts and trainers, so he delved into his suitcase to do likewise.

He couldn't even remember telling them he was staying at the Pheasant Hotel, but decided that he must have let it slip to Jacks during their get-to-know-each-other conversation earlier in the previous evening. He hoped that nothing else had slipped from his inebriated lips.

The pair was waiting in the lobby as Milton walked out of the lift, clutching a bottle of water in one hand and dabbing his leaking forehead with the other.

"Heavy night, Mr Milton?" Chalky asked in a voice imitating an Indian, accompanied by the wobbling head.

"Where are we going?" Milton enquired.

"You'll see," replied Stardust as the automatic exit doors opened and they entered the blinding sunshine outside.

It was almost too much for Milton, who covered his eyes. Chalky handed him a pair of Ray Bans.

"Cheers, mate," croaked Milton as he rushed them onto his nose.

In front of him were three four-wheel drives with their engines running and he could see Jacks was at the wheel of one, JT in another and the third was empty.

"Come this way. Your chariot awaits," said Stardust as they walked to the Range Rover that had been stuck in the sand two days earlier.

"Let's hope we don't get stuck anywhere today, hey Milton?" joked Chalky.

"Almost funny," Stardust replied abruptly.

Once they were in, they drove off in convoy through the city with Jacks leading at the front accompanied by Pups. JT was in the middle vehicle with Lenny and Kirk. Stardust was at the rear.

They inched their way through the busy Dubai streets before finding a stretch of highway that took them away from the city and towards the empty expanse of yellow sands stretching for miles towards the horizon.

Milton was starting to feel a little uneasy as he assessed his situation.

What if he had been rumbled? Gopal had told him of ghastly stories of people simply disappearing. He believed many people were murdered and dumped in the desert never to be found.

As the city Skyline faded away behind him, he became worried.

Maybe they were going to just put a bullet through his head. They were, after all, if the jobs advert was to be believed, former soldiers, and soldiers were trained to kill.

The butterflies in his stomach had now become the size of Tiger Moths. The desert road they were driving on was empty and he knew that if they wanted to kill him, they could do so at any time now and no one would ever find out.

His family would simply be told he had gone missing during an assignment and that would be it.

Not wanting to sound agitated, he leaned forward between the two front seats and asked, "Could you kindly tell me what we're doing?"

"Have you ever heard of dune driving or wadi bashing?" replied Chalky while looking at Stardust in the driving seat.

"Nope, but it sounds interesting."

Milton found some relief in the answer. He leaned back and started to enjoy the scenery, realising that his earlier fears were probably unfounded.

"You'd better buckle up tight, Milton. You'll be in for the experience of a lifetime in just a few minutes," said Stardust.

Milton hastily slid himself over to the corner of the back seat and attached the belt.

He looked ahead and saw Jacks, followed by JT, shoot off the road and onto the sands without slowing down. In fact, judging by the way the car left the first bump it looked as if they had accelerated.

Following the leader, Stardust increased his speed and set a course off the highway for the same dune that the previous two motors had disappeared over.

They approached it at over 40mph and Milton shouted in terror. "What the fuuuuuuuuu …"

The vehicle landed with an almighty crash about 15 feet on the down slope of a huge dune and continued to plummet downwards seemingly out of control.

Milton regained his senses and could see that Stardust was still steering the jeep and was accelerating down the hill even faster. They reached the base with a thud and again Milton was thrown about in the back seat. Without pausing, Stardust continued to drive in a straight direction up another sand mountain at about a 45-degree angle. Milton held on for dear life. The only things he was able to move were his eyeballs.

The Range Rover chewed up the sand and it still seemed to be accelerating as it hurtled off the top of the dune and landed on its front wheels on the other side. It bounced between its rear and front suspension before middling out on a flat piece of sand.

Milton was terrified and his hangover was soon forgotten.

The pair was screaming yahoos like American college kids and Milton was convinced his life was in the hands of two absolute maniacs.

The flat piece of land gave Milton time to regain his breath and ensure all his bodily parts were still in the right place. But it also allowed the vehicle to gain momentum again as it sped towards another blind ridge.

Milton held on tight as it hit the ridge at an angle and slid side-on all the way down the verge. Milton was sure the Range Rover was about to topple over, but Stardust wrestled with the steering wheel to ensure it remained steady.

They got to the bottom and Stardust performed a spectacular u-turn to finish with the rear of the Range Rover pointing towards another dune, which probably had yet another huge drop on the other side.

The three were breathing heavily and after a moment's pause Chalky looked at Stardust who said, "Let's do it!"

Stardust slipped the Range Rover into reverse and the jeep accelerated backwards.

"You have got to be kidding me!" was all Milton could muster before the Range Rover went flying over the dune and out of control through the air before crashing onto the downward slope.

As soon as it hit the base, Stardust thrashed on the handbrake and the Range Rover span round to face the front.

"Stop. Stop right now!" shouted Milton, struggling to regain his breath.

Stardust put his foot on the brake and Milton jumped out.

"You idiot, you could have killed us all," he shouted, as the two other jeeps pulled up.

His anger was met by laughter as the others found his reaction hilarious.

"Congratulations," said Jacks as he climbed from his motor. "You have now got a job at Expatriatedotcom."

Milton was now completely baffled.

"We need to know whether you've got balls and, to be honest, you stayed with Stardust and Chalky a lot longer than most of us would ever do. Welcome aboard."

Jacks reached out his hand and Milton, completely drained both mentally and physically, sniggered as he shook it steadily and then started to laugh out loud himself.

"Fuck you all," he said with a smile and the other men burst out laughing and joined the pair on the hot sands.

The rest of the morning was spent enjoying more sensible dune bashing before Jacks announced they should set up for lunch.

They arrived at a beautiful green oasis, which appeared out of the middle of the desert like a mirage. Even Beau Geste could not have hallucinated a more idyllic setting.

It was now midday and very hot, so they headed to a tented area that looked to be specially set up for tourists. A Bedouin welcomed them in and knew most of them by name. They walked into a carpeted tent that was lined with cushions and the men took off their shoes and stretched out.

"There's nothing like Bedouin hospitality," said Jacks. "They are the nicest people in the world. They have retained their heritage, and not moved into the city to live on big government handouts.

"Mohammed here has created a living out of entertaining tourists and he is doing well for himself."

Mohammed entered with a huge tray of food that the weary troops dived into. It was a mixed grill of meat accompanied by all the trimmings and it was some of the nicest grub Milton had tasted in a long time.

After eating, it was time for Milton to ask questions. He felt he had earned his right to do so.

"So when do I report for duty, sir?" he said, breaking the ice with a smile and a salute to his new officer in charge.

"Tomorrow is Thursday and the last day of our working week so why not start then. Give you a nice day to find your feet," said Jacks.

"I don't mean to be rude, but what exactly will I be doing and how much will I get?" Milton continued.

Jacks was unsure what role he wanted Milton to undertake just yet but he told him not to worry. His annual salary was 20,000 pounds tax-free, which would increase if he were promoted to special duties.

This interested Milton and he already reckoned he knew what these special duties were so he decided not to ask. He knew he would need to get through the promotional ladder fast. The England game in France was a month away and he was getting more confident that these men would be in the thick of it somewhere.

There were two things that didn't add up though.

Firstly, why would a cracking bunch of lads like this, obviously not short of money, become involved in football hooliganism?

Secondly, there had been no mention of football by any of them either last night or during the day.

Could he be barking up the wrong tree? Despite the pressure to produce results, Milton kind of hoped this was the case because he was beginning to like his new friends.

It was early afternoon by the time Milton arrived back at the hotel.

He was drained.

The past 24 hours had gone by like a blur.

It was now 2.00 p.m. and at this time yesterday he was wondering if he was ever going to get close to Carson Jacks. Now he had secured a job within the man's company and had in some strange way become his friend. He had enjoyed a damn good night out with him the previous night and a day in the desert that would have been many a tourist's dream.

He was either doing his job extremely well or was being set up. Milton would rather think the former. After all, he was now an experienced undercover operative and believed he had convinced his targets that he was a divorced ex-member of the Grenadier Guards that had become disillusioned with life in the UK and was looking for a lucky break in Dubai. It seemed to fit in with his new company's ethos.

There was no reason why anyone should doubt him and he felt the only way his cover could be blown was if one of the employees at Expatriatedotcom was an ex-Grenadier Guard and could find holes in his story. Even so, the dates he gave as his tours of duty equated with those obtained from the Regiment by Waite in the UK so he was confident.

He was exhausted but nevertheless he continued to read up on the city and went over his fantasy life story time and time again. The slightest crack and the operation, and his life, would be in jeopardy.

Chapter 12

Milton did not have a clue what was in store for him as the taxi dropped him off in front of the main doors of Expatriatedotcom.

It was just before midday and the sun was high in the sky. Milton curved his hand over his eyebrows to block its powerful rays from his eyes. He would at some point have to buy some sunglasses, he concluded.

The reception was unmanned, so he pressed the red button on the desk as the small sign instructed and sat close to the entrance door. Within seconds the big double doors opened and JT came barging through.

"Hi John, welcome to Expatriatedotcom," he said.

The pair shook hands and JT guided Milton through the doors and into the huge warehouse. He was met by shelves stacked with cardboard boxes of all sizes stretching right up to the ceiling. The warehouse appeared to be divided into numbered rows and he could see that the rows stretched to about 50 feet to the far wall.

This struck Milton as strange. From the outside he could see that the warehouse was at least 150 feet long but there appeared to be a segregating wall. He put it down to the company not requiring the full space and had simply hired the floor space required.

"I am the shift foreman this afternoon," JT explained to Milton, who had counted around 20 men busily working. All of them looked athletic and were aged between 25 and 40.

Everybody seemed friendly enough. JT introduced him to the staff as he walked past them and they replied with a handshake or a nod of the head and a smile.

"Expatriatedotcom was set up in 1996 by Carson," JT went on. "It got in at the right time. The Internet boom had begun and we just climbed on board the gravy train.

"What we provide is the cheapest patriotic stuff anywhere in the world. We ship out tens of thousands of national flags, t-shirts, mugs, caps … you name it and we'll see what we can do.

"In the run-up to the Millennium we were shipping it as soon as we received it. Every country in the world wanted to show its patriotism and we provided the cheapest solution. We were sending 10,000 flags at a time out to countries as diverse as the UK and Uzbekistan. We even received an order from the City of London for its Union Jack buntings!

"Things are obviously a little quieter these days, but we still make a living and Carson has looked after us all. He has never released a single employee despite the downturn.

"He has given you a job, not because we are busy but because he likes you. You'll be on special duties in no time!"

Milton was alerted.

"Special duties?" he asked.

"All in due time. But let's just say you are working for one of the most powerful firms in the world!"

A chill went down Milton's back. He knew he was in the thick of it now.

"So where's Carson?" asked Milton.

"He's away for a few days securing some contracts overseas. He should be back after the weekend."

JT explained to Milton what his job entailed. It was pretty mundane stuff. Basically, someone made an order over the Internet, the office processed it and a 'picker' - which was his job - took the order sheet, made it up on a cage and dropped it into the delivery bay. It was there that the order would be packed and dispatched by whichever way the orderer requested.

His shift was to be five hours, five days per week.

The work wasn't taxing and it allowed his mind to wander.

Milton just could not work it out. There must have been 20 men in that warehouse during his shift. Twenty men earning a minimum of 20 grand each. That comes to 400,000 pounds per year. Captain Ali had informed Waite last week that some 50 men were sponsored by the company. That would mean at least one million on wages alone.

Milton then looked at the vehicles in the car park through one of the large warehouse windows and concluded that some would have to be on considerably more than that to be able to afford the expensive sports cars and four-wheel drives he could see.

While people were busy moving around the warehouse, there seemed very few orders actually being filled.

JT said there had been boom years in the late '90s, but surely it is bad business to be retaining such a large staff if there's so little work and, more importantly, such little income coming in?

Milton enjoyed his work and managed to grab the odd word with his new colleagues who seemed pleasant enough.

Then a huge noise, like an air raid siren, sounded and everyone in the warehouse headed off in the same direction.

"What's happening, mate?" asked Milton, stopping a burly man with whom he had earlier exchanged pleasantries.

"Time for you to go home, new boy. That's the end of your day," he replied.

The five hours had passed by relatively quickly and Milton walked towards the staff room to wash up and grab his things.

Strangely, though, he found himself going against the pedestrian traffic flow. All the other workers were walking away from the staff room and towards the back of the building where the segregating wall stood.

He turned and peered from behind one of the rows of merchandise to see them heading towards a door, which was opened by the big figure of Lenny. Within seconds they had disappeared.

Milton, fearing he was missing out on something, scurried towards the door, which was pulled shut by Lenny after the last man walked through it.

"Sorry, John, not for you yet. Your day is over. Get yourself home and we'll see you on Sunday. Have a nice weekend," said Lenny with a wink as he stood in front of the door.

"No worries, Lenny, I just thought I was missing out on something," said Milton as he turned and walked through the derelict warehouse to the staff room.

He washed, grabbed his small bag, exited through the side door and got into a waiting taxi.

On his return to the hotel, Milton poured his thoughts onto paper and started to piece things together.

A few days earlier, when he was staking out the warehouse from Gopal's pick-up, he remembered seeing the employees walking in with sports bags shortly before midday. These were obviously the boys who had been on his shift. He had also seen men leave the building after 3.00 p.m. That was strange, so Milton drew up a wild theory.

Captain Ali had said some 50 men were sponsored by the company. What if they were split into two shifts, the first from 7.00 a.m. til midday and the second from 12.00 noon to 5.00 p.m? The men who worked the morning shift would then spend two or three hours doing something else in that segregated part of the warehouse and the same with the afternoon shift. If that were the case, then the men that Milton worked with on that day would depart the warehouse at 8.00 p.m.

He moved swiftly down to the taxi rank outside the hotel and returned to the warehouse. He was dropped off some distance away and maneuvered in the shadows towards it, close enough to view the side exit from where the workers departed.

Sure enough, just after 8.00 p.m. his colleagues from that afternoon started to file out, clutching their sports bags and in seemingly good spirits. Their jovial mood made it look as if they had just been playing five-a-side football. They had obviously done some sort of exercise that they enjoyed. They filtered out into the car park and dispersed in their collection of expensive motors.

Milton was convinced that whatever was going on in that segregated part of the warehouse was somehow linked to the wave of terror witnessed at England football matches across Europe.

A break-in was out of the question right now. The building was well guarded and he had not had time yet to find a way in. He was not willing to risk compromising his position just yet.

He had to get in there and there was an easier way of doing it.

Chapter 13

The weekend was spent liaising with London and reassuring them that he would have something soon.

Milton had been in Dubai a week and he could not believe how well it had gone. He passed every scrap of information on to Waite, who in turn briefed the team, but his superiors only needed to be reassured that things were going well.

He knew his team would never be pressurised into giving away information to the media, but he could not trust his coverage-hungry superiors. All it needed was one mention of the Middle East to an alert hack and his life would be in immediate danger. His bosses would only be told the bare essentials for the moment.

On the other hand, the dust had only just settled over Zurich and the France match was around the corner, less than a month away.

Milton was back in work on Sunday and decided his approach would be to show his keenness and to prove to his new employers that he was ready to take the step up. He had to know what else was going on at Expatriatedotcom and the only way he could do that would be through promotion.

Jacks was back in the office on the Monday and he had a brief chat with Milton, only revealing that his weekend business trip was fruitful.

Milton had asked Waite to tell Interpol to request the flight manifests over that weekend in and out of Dubai. They showed that Jacks had flown to Berlin. Nothing alarming there really, Milton thought. Business is business.

Tuesday night was spent with the lads again. It was another cracker.

At one point Kirk had been slapped by a blonde air hostess for a desperate chat-up line. His lines didn't always work, it seemed, but he operated on the process of elimination. Eventually one girl out there on a night out would fall for it and Kirk didn't give a toss what she looked like.

"Always go for the big girls. They appreciate it more and give you a far better time," he said before walking out of the bar with his arm stretched around the back of a huge Irish schoolteacher. She was so wide he could barely reach her other shoulder.

The cocktails flowed, it was a laugh a minute and a hangover was inevitable.

Pups was the target of a practical joke once again. This time he was chatted up by a beautiful young Russian girl.

"Well, lads, you have either got it or, in you sad bastards' case, you have not," was his goodbye to the lads as he headed for the exit with a smile that would make a Cheshire cat look miserable in comparison.

It was only after he had left arm in arm with the leggy brunette that Milton was told she was a prostitute who had already been paid for and organised by the lads.

"We have told her to tie him up, smear him in ice cream and then leave," said Stardust in his broadest Cockney voice. "Oh, and just for good measure we have told her to turn the air conditioning down as low as possible on the way out."

"We will nip over to his house in an hour and see him," added Chalky. "Don't want him dying of hypothermia now do we?"

Milton could not help but laugh and couldn't wait to join the lads when they went over to put Pups out of his misery. In fairness, the shivering Pups, covered in frozen chocolate and vanilla ice cream, saw the funny side of it once again and was still half expecting her to come back at some point.

"What are you doing here, lads?" was all he could muster through his chattering teeth when the mob burst into his freezing cold flat.

Wednesday dragged slower than a pregnant elephant being pulled by a mouse. Mind you, working days usually do when you are hungover.

By Thursday, Milton was becoming frustrated but he had to be patient. If he started asking questions about special duties it could raise suspicion, but time was running out.

It was now only three weeks until France entertained England and he was in trouble. He had got no nearer to the secrets of what lay behind that wall and the pressure was on for him to head back home to co-ordinate the anti-hooliganism operation for the game. He had put Waite in charge but his superiors were worried.

Milton knew there would be no returning to Dubai if he went back to the UK now. He just had to hope that he would be embraced into the special duties soon.

Thursday provided his big break.

As the clock dragged towards 5.00 p.m., Milton was called into Jacks's office.

"Sit down, Milton," said Jacks.

The office was nothing special and contained no personal pictures or souvenirs. It was, in fact, painfully dull.

"JT tells me you've been doing an exceptional job over the last week, Milton," opened Jacks.

"Thanks, Carson. I've enjoyed the work and I can't thank you enough for sorting me out." Milton knew this was leading to somewhere and wanted to kiss as much ass as possible.

"C'mon, man, you can't fool me. The job's boring and you seem an intelligent man. You could do this with your eyes shut."

Jacks climbed from his seat and put his hands in his pockets as he looked out of the window.

He then changed his tone, using Milton's Christian name for what seemed like the first time. "What do you think about the UK these days, John?"

"What do you mean?"

"I mean, why are you here and not living in England when you once swore to Queen and country that you would quite gladly give your life to defend its shores?"

Milton was shocked. It was a question that came from out of the blue and somehow he felt Jacks was testing him out.

"To be honest with you, Carson," Milton paused for breath, "I feel a little let down by England, but I would still do anything to protect it."

Jacks walked from behind the desk and stood over Milton, who started to feel uneasy. What if he had just insulted what Jacks believed in? These could be the last breaths that he would ever take.

Jacks extended his hand and added, "Welcome aboard, John. I think you are ready to join us for special duties."

Jacks made a quick phone call and Stardust entered the office with Chalky.

"He's ready boys," Jacks said.

"I knew it from the minute I met him in that sand pit," said Stardust as he patted Milton on the back.

"I think you fancy him," replied Chalky.

"Why, are you jealous, gay boy?" said Stardust as the two exchanged play punches and ushered Milton out of the door.

Milton was still completely in the dark and did not have a clue as to what he was letting himself in for.

As the three walked away from the office, Stardust and Chalky led Milton towards the door that allowed access to the segregated area at the back of the warehouse.

The air siren, signalling the end of the afternoon shift, had sounded while Milton was chatting in Jacks's office, so the warehouse was already deserted.

A wild river of adrenalin was flowing through Milton as Lenny stood aside and allowed the three to enter what had previously represented the unknown for Milton.

He was absolutely numbed by what he saw.

In front of him was one of the most well-equipped gymnasiums he had ever set his eyes on. There were cycling machines, treadmills, weight benches and enough free weights to sink a ship.

"What the hell is this place?" Milton said as his eyes struggled to absorb everything in front of him.

"What's wrong, John?" said Chalky, patting Milton's stomach. "Have you never seen a gym before?"

"This is where you will work from 5.00 p.m. to 6.00 p.m. after your shift finishes. Expatriatedotcom is a very caring company and we like all our employees to be in good shape," Stardust explained with a laugh.

Milton could see that Pups appeared to be the main fitness coach, putting men through their paces on the huge array of machines.

Milton's guided tour continued. Behind a small segregation panel of around 10 feet, there were a number of punchbags hanging from beams and mats laid out on the floor.

"This is where you will work from 6.00 p.m. to 7.00 p.m., John. Let's just say we will sharpen up your self-defence here," said Stardust as he looked and laughed at Chalky.

Milton stood and watched in amazement as Kirk and JT were training three men in what looked like martial art techniques on one of the mats.

As they watched, Lenny came from behind them and launched a volley of punches into one of the punchbags that was being catapulted in every direction.

"All that martial art stuff is for puffs," he exclaimed, showing his clenched fist to Milton. "Brute strength and a knockout punch are what's needed these days."

"Needed for what?" Milton enquired.

"Ah," said Chalky as if they had forgotten something. "Your final hour at work is spent in here."

They walked past the mat as Kirk decked one of the 'students' with a judo throw over his shoulder.

Chalky opened a door and the trio entered what resembled a classroom. There were around 50 desks facing a blackboard. To the right of that was a huge television screen linked up to a video and other electronic boxes, which Milton immediately recognised from his own high-tech surveillance equipment in his briefing office in London.

It was astonishing. Jacks was training a bloody army.

He looked around the room in astonishment as Stardust and Chalky fiddled with the electronic equipment.

Outside he could hear the thud of the combat training on the mats and the grunts and groans of the men in the gym.

If, as he suspected, all of the employees of Expatriatedotcom were ex-British military, Jacks had at his disposal a complete militia.

The thought left Milton speechless. What had he stumbled across here?

As he shook his head in disbelief, a voice came from the direction of the door: "Park your arse, John, it is time to start your education."

He turned to see Jacks enter the room and flick on the lights.

"You two can park up too. You could do with a refresher." He motioned to Stardust and Chalky who sat either side of Milton at the three desks in the middle of the second row.

"John. We have all been very impressed by your progress and you have a lot to offer this organisation.

"You are one of us. You talk like us, you think like us and you feel let down by your country like us but, as you said, you would still do anything to protect it."

Milton just sat and nodded in acknowledgement, still dumbstruck as everything unfolded around him.

Jacks patrolled the room from left to right.

"We all have one thing in common here, John. We are all fiercely proud of being English. We love England and would do anything to defend it.

"But we won't live there, and why? Because we have been let down by what is happening there. A regime that has turned its back on the ordinary people.

"England, because it is the greatest nation on Earth, has become a dumping ground for what comes out of the arse of other countries.

"We have become sympathetic to the needs of everyone else, and the needs of those actually living there have become second fiddle.

"We are not racist thugs, John. You can leave that to the Nazi idiots. We are talking plain common sense. Of course everyone wants to come to England to live, it is the best country in the world. All we are saying is, take in those who can actually offer something to enhance the nation.

"I do feel sorry for the asylum seekers who leave their countries because their lives are in danger. But imagine all the young men in Britain that thought their lives were in danger in 1939 had set sail to the Americas instead of standing firm to fight.

"Some of those same men are now having to sell up their houses and go to places like Germany to pay for operations and medical treatment. If they joined the hospital waiting lists in England they would be dead before their turn came around.

"We have opened our arms to the world, and our hospitality - or stupidity - has been abused.

"The people of England are losing hope and becoming a nation of Saturday night fighters, drug addicts and benefit scroungers.

"But that will not go on for ever, John. Don't worry, the honest man's day will come again and we will regain control of our country.

"As you may have gathered by now, John, we are all ex-servicemen. Most have come here through recommendations and others have applied via the Internet. For every man here, John, there are another 10,000 who would want to be here.

"All of these men still want to fight for the country of their birthplace but can't tolerate living there and seeing what it has become.

"We live the life of Riley out here, John, as you know. We are all trained to fight for our country and we do it in a way that shows how patriotic England still is, and it sends a clear message across the world telling people that we have had enough." Jacks paused to draw breath, then continued.

"Did you see the pictures on television of the trouble in Switzerland a couple of weeks back, John?"

Milton nodded only, not wanting to knock Jacks off his soapbox.

"What did you think, John, when you saw hundreds of fans proudly flying the St George flag and wreaking havoc? What message did that send to you through the media?"

Milton had a feeling that he knew where this was heading. He wanted to say it sent out a message that had ruined his life for the past year but he continued to play along.

"It made me think that England has gone wild. It made me think that the country is angry; aggressive and hostile towards anything non-English."

"Bingo," continued Jacks.

"And that is the message we want to get through to people hoping to come to our country to abuse our system.

"Those men you saw on television are the ordinary men on the street; the ones that are paying high taxes to supplement illegal immigrants - people on the dole, benefit frauds, I could list them for hours.

"Football provides those people with a platform to show off their patriotism, vent their frustrations while at the same time fight for their country.

"For sure, those men are pretty sad too. They tank themselves up on beer and can barely swing their tattooed arms past their inflated bellies."

Jacks paused again and changed direction to walk to the window, looking out to the men training.

"But these men here have fought for their country," he continued. "Many of these men, like Chalky and Stardust here, fought with me in the Gulf War. Some are Special Forces, some are squaddies, some are engineers and some are communications experts.

"What we have here, John, is an elite version of the British Army. Men who thought they had a job for life but became disillusioned with it for some reason or another and bailed out.

"They have come to realise that soldiers this day and age no longer fight for their Queen and country. They fight for politicians to win votes, putting their lives on the line in shitholes like Iraq just for some public schoolboy to gain some popularity - using good men's lives for convincing people to put the cross in the right place on a ballot paper once every four years."

Milton was absolutely dumbstruck and simply continued to listen, motionless.

"Here they have that job for life, John. They have a family in each other and they have a group of people who will stick by them through thick and thin. The only thing they miss is England as it was, but we will all return home one day.

"That day will come when the country is strong once again - when we are revered across the world as a powerful nation and not a soft touch."

Jacks looked Milton straight in the eye and was gauging every blink, twitch or movement. Milton knew he was in the spotlight and kept listening intently. Jacks again cast his gaze back towards his men training hard outside.

"These men have skills of warfare and confrontation. What we do here is hone those skills and use them in a different confrontational situation.

"Football is our battlefield, John. We are proud Englishmen and we need to get our buzz from what we are trained in."

Milton was transfixed to his every word.

"Do you think these men joined the army to overlook miles of nothingness in Germany from watchtowers? Or march off into the Arabian desert on meaningless exercises in the hope that maybe one day they might actually see some action?

"No, John, the buzz comes from confrontation and putting into practice what you have been trained to do. The extra buzz comes from seeing the successful implementation of all that training come to life on TV."

Milton continued to play dumb. "But I saw on the news that all this trouble is ruining England's chances of staging the World Cup in 2006?" he said.

"Exactly," replied Jacks. "The World Cup is watched by billions of people across the world. This tournament will make England the most desirable destination in the world for any asylum seeker or scrounger looking for the greener grass on the other side.

"In 1966, John, when England last staged the World Cup, we still ruled over half the world and were a bigger superpower than the USA, Russia or China will ever be. Then it was all about Britain and Britishness. You were privileged to be let in to such a great country.

"Look at us now, a downtrodden nation relying on a sporting event to lift the country's spirits. No, John, there's plenty of time for the world's attention to be on England and 2006 I am afraid is too soon.

"A World Cup in England will just encourage more people to go and live there. That's the last thing we want."

Milton took it all in and couldn't decide whether Jacks was a genius or a madman. Whichever way, he was a genius or a lunatic with his own mini-militia at his disposal.

He had hand-picked a group of men, provided them with well-paid jobs in paradise and allowed them to continue what they loved most: fighting for their country.

Brilliant. Simply brilliant.

"So then, John, are you in or are you out?" Jacks rested a hand on Milton's shoulder.

Milton climbed from his seat, knowing he had no option at all. "I'm in. One hundred and ten per cent."

His answer was hailed by pats on the back from Stardust and Chalky as Jacks walked to the door and back into the gym.

"Oh, and by the way, John," he added as he turned before departing, "you've got a pay rise. Fifty thousand pounds per year. Congratulations."

Bloody hell, Milton thought.

Chapter 14

The weekend was spent in the Pheasant Hotel where Milton had decided to stay for the time being rather than move into an apartment. He was confident that by remaining in a hotel his phone calls couldn't be monitored and he regularly swept his room for listening devices.

Jacks and his army were true professionals and he couldn't afford to leave anything to chance.

Milton couldn't get his head around the fact that he was now earning 50,000 quid per year tax free. How on earth could Jacks afford it? There certainly wasn't enough revenue coming through Expatriatedotcom to pay all that money to so many men.

It was not surprising that the men were so happy. Not one of them was paying taxes, so they were pocketing more money than the average cabinet minister.

The mathematics just didn't add up. Milton would somehow have to tap into the financial records of the company, but only one man was in control of them and that was Jacks.

"Jacks runs the whole financial side of the company. We're just happy picking up our bucks at the end of the month and he hasn't let any of us down yet," Stardust had said earlier in the week.

Milton was invited to spend a wild weekend away with a few of the lads from the company, but decided he wanted to get things straight in his own mind. The whole situation was moving along at an alarming pace and he wanted to go over all the events of the past two weeks to ensure he was still in control.

France was just three weeks away and surely they would be planning their operation soon. Maybe they had started it already.

Milton had been in Dubai now for three weeks and, despite the initial culture shock, he was enjoying his time there. The city had so much to offer and he thrived in the climate.

Most of the weekend's mulling was done by the hotel pool and his occasional trip out of the hotel was to the magical souks and markets sprinkled across the city.

He scarcely thought of the wife and kids back home and each time he tried to call he reached the answering machine. His private life appeared to be in tatters but out here it didn't matter. He had struck up new friendships and was earning more money than he could ever possibly hope to achieve in the force.

Life was getting a little too cosy for Milton in Dubai, a fact that he was reminided of in a telephone conversation with Waite.

"How are things going?" asked Milton over the phone.

"Very well, sir, but the chief is getting anxious," he replied.

"What do you mean?"

"He wants you here, sir. They all want you here."

"Waite, I'm relying on you. You've got to be a reassuring figure. If I leave Dubai now we will never get to the bottom of this. They are planning something big, Waite, for France and, believe me, we will be helpless to stop it unless I'm on the inside."

Waite seemed convinced but simply wanted to put his boss in the picture.

"They think you're having a holiday, sir," he said after a small pause.

There was another silence on the phone as a temper boiled from within Milton. If only they could see how he had put his life on the line, all for a job at the end of the day. Having said that, he had just spent the best part of the last 48 hours at the hotel swimming pool.

"Sod 'em, Waite. Sod 'em all. We will crack this case if it is the last thing we ever do. I need you to be strong, Waite. Don't worry about me, everything will be fine."

Milton hung up, knowing his operation balanced on a knife edge. He ordered a conference call with Deputy Assistant Commissioner Dobson and his colleagues. He knew it could be his last chance to prolong his Dubai operation. He feared the worst and was sure that they would order him to return home and back to the helm of the task force.

Luckily for Milton, his biggest fan, Commissioner Sir Michael Bryers, was in on the conference call too. If Dobson were the top-ranking officer there he would for sure be on the next flight west.

Milton spilled the beans for the first time and gave a complete report on what was happening at Expatriatedotcom and Carson Jacks. He named Jacks as the man in charge of the operation and the single most dangerous threat to England's chances of staging the World Cup in 2006.

As Milton went on, the interruptions became less frequent; a sign that his audience was as shocked as he first was at the revelations.

Sir Michael tried to conclude by saying, "So what you are saying, John, is that this Jacks fella has trained an army in football hooliganism?"

"Well, in a nutshell, sir, yes."

To substantiate his claims, Milton referred to the alleged anti-globalisation camps set up in parts of Europe and the USA to train eco-warriors and the like.

"But why on earth would someone who believes he is so patriotic do such a thing?"

Milton went on to paraphrase the sermon that Jacks had delivered a couple of days earlier and described him as a character similar to Timothy McVeigh, the former US soldier who became disillusioned with his government and carried out the Oklahoma City bombing.

"This man is smart and has an army eating out of the palm of his hand," explained Milton.

Milton could hear chatter on the other end of the phone line and presumed that Sir Michael was holding some kind of response forum with his officers.

"Milton, well done. You have carried out some stunning work over there. What assistance can we give you now?" offered Sir Michael.

Milton knew he had just won a personal battle. They were 100 per cent behind him now.

"Sir, I just need a bit more time. At the moment they have not even mentioned the France game so I need to gather more intelligence," he explained.

"Do you want us to contact the authorities in Dubai? Surely we have enough evidence to close this man down now, do we not?" Sir Michael asked.

"No, sir. For some reason, a member of the local ruling family sponsors this company and anything under their umbrella is untouchable. I do not know how this man has done it, but he is basically above the law here."

This particular piece of news raised a huge red flag. Could they be facing an international diplomatic incident too?

Concerned, Sir Michael requested clarification. "Are you saying, John, that the Dubai Government is sponsoring football hooliganism?"

Not wanting his boss to be misled, Milton replied with confidence, "No, sir, I am sure that is not the case. Far from it. Somehow his company is running under their sponsorship but I am confident that their operations are completely independent. I am not even considering that option. Sir, in my opinion, the Dubai ruling family is completely oblivious to this and has no idea what they are up to. I am sure they would have closed them down if they knew."

Sir Michael seemed relieved. "Do carry on, John," he said.

"Thank you, sir. We have run international checks on Carson Jacks and we have run checks with the military, navy and air force and have unearthed nothing so far on neither him nor his men. I can only conclude that he is living under a fresh identity here. I have a lot more work to do here and I request more time, sir. There are too many loose ends. I desperately need more time."

Milton waited while his bosses chatted amongst themselves on the other end of the line. He couldn't quite hear what was being said but felt confident.

"Request granted, John. Please do keep us informed. Time is running out."

Milton breathed a huge sigh of relief on hanging up. He could now concentrate on the job at hand without the nuisance of worrying about work on the ground in France. That was entirely in Waite's hands now and he was confident his young sergeant was up to the challenge.

Chapter 15

For the first time Milton felt he was now well and truly absorbed into Expatriatedotcom. He went to work with a kitbag over his shoulder just like the other men and was looking forward to his shift concluding at 5.00 p.m. when his special duties would commence.

The day flew by and it wasn't long before Milton was entering the back of the warehouse and changing into his gym wear.

Pups put him through his paces: first the exercise bike, then the treadmill and then the weights. Milton hadn't gone through a session like it since first joining the police force.

He didn't have long to recover. Pups handed him over to Kirk who took him through some basic self-defence. None of this was new to Milton. The force had taught him everything he needed to know in self-defence and he had put it to the test on plenty of occasions.

Then came his classroom session after a quick shower and change. Not surprisingly, Jacks was the teacher.

As the class of about 20 'students' settled into their seats, Jacks scrolled down a city map over the blackboard.

"This is the beautiful city of Paris," he said with a welcoming swish of his arm and an open palm in the direction of the map.

Milton looked around the classroom and could see his work colleagues were fixated on every word Jacks preached.

He explained the various suburbs of the city as Stardust handed out smaller versions of the map to everyone present.

"Tomorrow is Monday and myself and Chalky will head off to Paris for a couple of days of sightseeing. We will be back here on Thursday and by then I want you all to be familiar with this map. Learn the street names, the landmarks, the location of the stadium and, if you want, buy a beret and a string of onions for disguise."

The classroom erupted into laughter as Jacks rolled up the giant map and announced, "Dismissed."

"That was harmless enough," Milton commented, turning to Pups who was seated to his right and folding up his map before popping it into a pocket in his bag.

"Wait until next week when we start planning the operation," said Pups. "We'll be in here for an hour solid each night. By the end of next week, you could work as a tour guide of Paris, believe me!"

Milton had targeted Pups as a possible weak link in the group. He suspected that Pups was not ex-military and he was by far the youngest member of the whole outfit by some margin. Most of the lads were in their thirties; Pups had the features of a kid just out of high school.

He was a good kid. Milton often wondered how on earth he had got mixed up in this whole situation and decided it was time to get to know him a lot better.

"So how did you end up here, Pups?" Milton asked as the two walked to the car park shoulder to shoulder. Milton was reluctant to ask too many questions to some of the older members just in case it aroused suspicion. Pups, he gambled, was different.

"It's a long story, Milton," he replied. "What you up to now?"

Milton just shrugged as if to say nothing much.

"C'mon, John, let's go and shoot some pool. I could do with a beer."

Milton jumped into Pups's car, a Fiat Coupe, which roared out of the car park and back onto the highway. They didn't speak much in the car, mainly due to Pups's erratic driving, and eventually arrived at a city centre hotel.

They walked into the bar. Pups was well known to the staff, who plonked two Budweisers on the bar as he arrived.

"I hope you don't mind drinking the King of Beers?" he said, handing one of the bottles to Milton and directing him towards a pool table. "It's the best tonic for playing pool."

Pups racked up the balls and invited Milton to break.

"So, Pups, how did you end up here? I mean, you seem to be a lot younger than the other guys and I will place my neck on the chopping block to say you have not been in the forces."

"Is it that obvious?" Pups thrashed a ball into the bottom right pocket and chalked his cue.

"Carson Jacks is a hell of a guy, Milton," he said as he arched down for another pot. "Do you actually know anything about him?"

"Not a bean. He did tell me he served in the Gulf War but that was about it."

Pups potted another ball and moved around the table, chalking his cue as he swiftly manoeuvred to take another shot.

"Carson served with my brother in the Gulf War. They were best friends in their army days and were like brothers."

Pups came up from a shot and hitched his bottom up to sit on the corner of the pool table facing Milton, who sat next to a small round table and cradled his beer. He leaned towards Pups, not wanting to miss a word.

"I was 12 when the Gulf War was on. I was hearing all these stories about Iraq being bombarded from the air and that ground troops would not be used. Every day I was glued to that television watching the developments.

"My brother was there, operating with some Special Forces unit. He never did say which one; all we knew was that he was out there somewhere. We knew Carson was there too, as they had both been to our house for dinner before saying they were heading out there. This was soon after the invasion of Kuwait and weeks before the air strikes started.

"They never said where they were going, only that it was a mission and it was somewhere in the Middle East. We just presumed it was either Iraq or Kuwait.

"My brother was 23, the same as Carson, and he was my hero. He was like a father figure to me because I never knew my father. I idolised him and cried for a week when he left."

Pups prised himself off the table and onto the floor. He circled the table and eyed up his next shot.

"Then we got the news a few weeks into the conflict. We received a phone call from Carson saying my brother had been killed during the operation and his body could not be recovered. They had simply buried him in the desert in Kuwait."

He paused and put the pool cue down, then picked up his beer and leaned against the table adjacent to Milton.

"My mother was never the same again. She died three years later, and as soon as I left school I joined Carson out here in Dubai. He was like a big brother and a father to me. He had promised my brother that he would look after me and that is exactly what he has done.

"He put me through college over here and I got a diploma in sports science. I am now a specialist physical trainer and I owe it all to Carson. If it weren't for him, I'm sure I would have ended up in trouble in some way in the UK. I had lost all direction. Carson gave me a life and for that I am eternally grateful."

It was a moving story. Jacks was a hero to all the men at Expatriatedotcom and had earned their respect.

Milton was touched. He had grown to admire Jacks over the weeks and could see how he had become such a dominant father figure to them all. But his suspicion that Pups could be a weak link had been proved right and his subtle probing had to continue.

"I don't understand though, Pups. Why was it Carson who told you that your brother was dead and not the Ministry of Defence or the military?" asked Milton.

The youngster took a gulp from his bottle, wiped his lips and continued.

"My brother and Carson were no longer in the army. Both had left three months earlier and were working as mercenaries, or soldiers of fortune if you like.

"They never really told us why they had left. My brother just said the army was not rewarding men like him and Carson enough and they could earn more money 'freelancing' as he liked to call it.

"It was all very sudden when they left the army and we were not sure what exactly had happened. My brother and Carson never really liked to talk about it so we never mentioned it. A need to know thing, I guess you could call it, and they decided that we didn't need to know.

"Carson met a lot of the guys here through the Gulf War. Many of them were doing the same as him, recruited for special missions by the Saudi and Kuwaiti royals to recover members of their families who had been kidnapped by Iraqi forces or stranded behind enemy lines.

"The British Government denied their existence and never even acknowledged the death of my brother, nor the deaths of dozens of other men like him. People like my brother and Carson did more to win the Gulf War than any US or British air strikes and yet their existence was denied."

Milton was intrigued and wanted to find out more. He felt he had gained the trust of Pups and had to pursue the conversation further.

"So how on earth did the company start up?" he said.

Pups, getting over his emotional tale, returned to the game and continued to clean up the table.

"It's usually left to Jacks to tell you this in the classroom, but I guess he won't mind me filling you in. After all, he's going to be busy over the next few weeks."

Pups slammed in the black ball and joined Milton by the table in the corner of the room.

"People like Carson and my brother were labelled as bounty hunters by the British Government and were simply disowned. The mission in which my brother was killed was to rescue a young Arab sheikh who was visiting Kuwait from Dubai when the country was invaded.

"The sheikh was held under arrest in the palace he was visiting but his family feared for his safety. Carson and my brother joined five others and went in to rescue him. It was a success but three were gunned down, including my brother.

"Carson and the others were stranded in Kuwait for weeks, shielding the sheikh from thousands of Iraqi troops searching for them.

"The Iraqi propaganda machine, wanting to cover up the public relations disaster of losing the sheikh and being unable to track them down, said they had foiled a Special Forces assault and gunned down all of the men.

"With no news of their welfare, and certainly no details of their mission, the embarrassed British Government simply said the men were money-hungry mercenaries killed in action.

"It was easier for the West to deny that such a mission had ever taken place. In fact they weren't even aware of it, so they said. Such missions were causing the Coalition a lot of problems, as they were struggling to get their resources into the region quick enough to launch their own missions.

"They eventually returned the sheikh to Dubai and were treated behind closed doors as war heroes by the Government and ruling family. The survivors, including Chalky and Stardust, felt betrayed by their own British Government and were offered the chance to live in Dubai.

"It was a difficult decision for Carson because he, like the other men, are fiercely patriotic, but they were offered the chance to start afresh so they agreed.

"The ruling family feared assassination attacks after the Gulf War, so Carson headed up a specialist royal protection group. He recruited former servicemen he could trust who in turn trained the local army.

"By the time I got here in 1996, the threat from Iraq had receded and the area was actually going into recession due to the dropping oil prices. The royals decided that the local soldiers Carson's men had trained provided sufficient protection, so his unit was surplus to requirement.

"He had his own private army but no one to fight for. None of the men wanted to return home and feared they would be left in no-man's-land. Many feared they could be arrested for being mercenaries. Up the creek without a paddle I think the phrase is. Carson himself had long turned his back on the

UK and was in no rush to come back from the dead after so long.

"Anyway, Carson pleaded with the sheikh he had saved five years earlier to intervene and he offered him the opportunity of running a business under his sponsorship so they could stay in the country as residents.

"Hence Expatriatedotcom. He gave every single one of his men a job and good wages to keep them happy. The sheikh bankrolled the first couple of years and then the business took off for the millennium."

It still didn't make sense to Milton though; how did this lot get involved in football hooliganism? He posed the question to Pups in between two huge gulps of beer.

"While we were okay earning big bucks and living the lifestyle, it soon became obvious to Carson that not everyone was getting job satisfaction and some were talking about leaving.

"Even Carson himself was fed up. I mean, you have got to understand, John; all that these men knew was fighting and confrontation. Now they were pushing trollies around a warehouse assembling mail orders requests. They missed the buzz and so did Carson just as much as any of them.

"In 1998, two years back, we all held a big meeting and chatted about things. At first people were too scared to mention their unrest to Carson - after all, he was their idol and hero figure - but he just came out with it.

"'Football,' he said, and everyone just sat there in bemusement thinking he was going to be introducing a soccer team or something to improve morale.

"'Anyone ever been to a football match?' I remember him saying. He then went on to preach to us about the state of Britain and how we could be the saviours simply by organising a network of terror at England football matches abroad.

"At first everyone was sceptical but, as always, they listened to every word Carson said. He told them that England needed to stand tall, push back its shoulders and puff out its chest to the world once again.

"He struck a nerve. All the lads had seen comrades killed fighting for their country and Carson made them believe that they could be responsible for making Britain proud again.

"All the lads are trained in something, Carson just adapted everyone's techniques towards the football environment. He basically breathed life into a decaying fighting machine."

Milton absorbed every word that came from Pups's mouth. Little did the youngster realise that he had just told Milton enough to lock up his idol, Jacks, and the rest of the men for a very long time. It was priceless information but useless because Milton did not have anything to record it with.

It was brilliant though, the way it had come about. From disenchanted squaddies to expatriate playboys seeing themselves as the men to put the 'great' back into Britain. This really was huge. It had to be true because you could not make up such a story.

So incredible was the tale that Milton had not noticed Pups order two more beers which crashed down on the table with a thud.

Milton still needed to find out more about Jacks's background but he did not want to push his luck too far with Pups. His answers would have to come from the man himself. He had to get inside the head of Carson Jacks.

Chapter 16

Working at Expatriatedotcom had taken on a whole new meaning for Milton. Pups had provided him with exactly what he was looking for; now he needed to work out a way to gather evidence in order to smash the group.

But that was not going to be easy. Firstly, it had become apparent very early on to Milton that Jacks was very much in command and told his foot soldiers only what they needed to know. Secondly, Milton was enjoying life like he had never enjoyed life before. He was alive and had regained a thirst for fun which had all but dried up through years of mundane family life, not to mention the rigours of and sacrifices for his job. He had built up close friendships with his new work colleagues and felt part of a family, something he had not felt for some time back home.

Dubai was indeed a city that was young and vibrant. Every night was legendary and better than the previous one. There was always something to do in the evenings and the weekends were spent basking under the gorgeous autumn sun. Milton had acquired a taste for the expatriate life and it was something he did not particularly want to let go of, just yet.

Smashing this ring would mean the likes of Jacks, Stardust, Chalky, Lenny, Kirk, JT and Pups would be put away for a very long time. It was something he didn't wish to contemplate and it sometimes took a phone call to Waite back at HQ to remind him which side he was actually on.

Pups had told him plenty but not enough and he didn't want to probe him any further. Otherwise he might actually start sounding like a policeman again.

Milton had to get close to the men that knew Jacks best and that would have to be either Stardust or Chalky, the men Jacks had known the longest and served with in the Gulf War. If Pups was right, these three had spent weeks behind enemy lines in Kuwait saving each other's lives on a daily basis. If that did not make them close then nothing could.

With Jacks and Chalky out of the country in Paris, presumably planning ahead, Stardust was placed in charge of the company. With a stroke of luck,

Milton was paired with Stardust during a post-work workout on the Tuesday night.

"You know, Stardust, coming to work here makes me realise just how much I missed the craic in the regiment," he said as the two stretched off at the end of the hour.

"You/me the same, mate, you/me the same," replied Stardust as he poured a cold bottle of water over his sweat-drenched hair.

"What was it like in the Gulf War, Stardust? I joined too late and they were rounding up the Iraqis by the time I came out of basic training."

"It was tough, mate," Stardust replied, handing Milton a sports drink.

"I had left the army a year earlier. I was in the Royal Signals and specialised in communications. I did four years' training and you know where they stationed me? The Falkland Islands.

"I did three years of looking at sheep from our base and I might as well have become a Buddhist monk for all the shagging I did. I decided to see it through because I was seconded to the Special Forces when they were conducting exercises on the islands. I dedicated myself to my job because there was fuck-all else to do.

"I was close to going nuts, Milton. Every day I got out of bed; went to the office; went to the mess for a few beers with the other hairy arses; and then back to bed. Some life for a lad in his early 20s eh?

"My tour of duty approached its conclusion and guess where they decided to send me? A listening-in intelligence centre on the Orkney Islands!

"I couldn't face it, spending hours sifting through phone calls and trying to intercept anything that might be of use.

"I bailed out quick sticks. I got in touch with a couple of the Special Forces fellas that I had served with in the Falklands and one was Chalky who had just left the SAS. He had been in for three years and had decided to work as a shadow for rich Arabs holidaying in London."

"A shadow?" asked Milton.

"Yeah, you know. A bodyguard or minder. He was getting paid twice as much for walking around hotels with some rich Arab kids and making sure they got a taxi home okay at the end of the night. He put in the word for me and I joined him. It was easy money all right but I was itching to get back into communications.

"Then the invasion happened. One of the Arabs we had been shadowing in London was kidnapped in Kuwait and we got the call-up. We were offered big money and both of us were keen to get back into what we had been trained to do.

"We arrived in Dubai and met Carson in a hotel and he told us the plan. You could tell immediately that this geezer was the dog's chestnuts, so we put our trust in him 100 per cent. We were getting paid well to do it but he made sure we knew the risks.

"A week later, after a little desert training, we were off. We met Kuwaiti resistance fighters at the border with Saudi who smuggled us into Kuwait City. The place was a mess and there were men being executed in the streets in front of their own families. It was terrible.

"We spent five days in hiding and were able to obtain accurate plans of the building where the sheikh was being held. Then we moved in. The place was heavily guarded. There were seven of us and we reckon we took out at least 40 of them. They were poorly trained soldiers but heavily armed and three of our men were cut down.

"Carson refused to leave the bodies behind. We had seen what they had done with the dead. The strung them up and cut off the skin on their chests to attract the birds to eat them in the streets.

"We got out of the building and were assisted by dozens of Kuwaiti resistance fighters on the streets who fought a whole garrison of Iraqi troops right through the night so we could get clear. We managed to get to the safe house and buried the three dead in the desert.

"We were stranded. Our Kuwaiti friends reckoned up to 5,000 Iraqi soldiers were looking for us. This number of soldiers being reassigned from the front line to search for us probably saved hundreds if not thousands of lives too. We were moving every day and spent more nights than not sleeping in pipes, drains, under scrub, in fact anywhere that gave us cover. It was nearly a month until we made it out across the border and into Saudi Arabia.

"It was one hell of a mission, Milton, but there were no medals or promotions waiting for us when we got out. British army generals denied the raid had taken place and we were all officially listed as dead or missing in action. The British Government branded us as gold-digging mercenaries, which I suppose we were, but they also said men like us were doing more harm than good to their war effort. It was devastating and none of us wanted to go back to the UK after that.

"But Carson came to the rescue though and the rest, as they say, is now history."

Milton could tell that Stardust was bitter about the whole thing and so he chose his next words wisely.

"You know what, Stardust?" he said. "Sometimes people are never grateful."

The two nodded their heads and looked to the floor before they burst out laughing.

"Sod 'em all," said Stardust. "It is time for me to kick your arse next door."

The pair got to their feet and headed for their next hour of combat training with JT and Kirk on the mats.

* * *

It was bizarre, but no one seemed to know anything about Jacks before 1991, before the Gulf War. Pups only knew that he had served with his brother, but the vagueness of his account could either be put down to his being so young at the time or to the fact that the pair was in the Specials Forces and reluctant to talk about it.

Judging by what Stardust had said about the operation in Kuwait and the way he ran the business in Dubai, the latter seemed the most likely, but there were no military records for a Carson Jacks. Waite had requested the Ministry of Defence to look time and time again but to no avail. It must be a false name and he had to find out for sure his real identity.

His chance would come on the Saturday night. Jacks and Chalky returned from their trip to Paris on the Thursday, Chalky in the morning and then Jacks in the evening. Jacks had had to fly back via Germany to tie up a few loose ends for the business deal he was working on two weeks earlier.

Chalky stormed into the warehouse in his usual indomitable fashion and was soon taking the piss out of his favourite targets.

"How was the trip, geezer?" asked Stardust in typical Cockney English.

"You'll be glad to know, Stardust, that Paris is indeed gay and you and your hairy rear are in for a great time!"

Stardust joined in the laughter. He had no choice really, as Chalky was always quicker to release the witty one-liners.

Chalky called a meeting of all the staff and handed out an envelope to everyone.

He said, "As we're such a caring company and as we're going to be very busy over the next couple of weeks, we have decided to throw a barbecue this Saturday night at our compound. Feel free to bring a partner and as much booze as you like!"

The invite was warmly accepted by the lads. Milton slid his finger under the envelope flap and ripped it open. Inside were his open invitation and a map on how to get to the venue.

He had worked hard all week, he thought to himself, so a party was exactly what he deserved.

Chapter 17

The smell of barbecued food that filled his nostrils was indication enough that Milton had reached the correct destination for the party.

His taxi driver had put on the usual tiresome act of not knowing where he was going despite the help of Stardust's map, but Milton had been in Dubai long enough now to know the general direction.

He could hear the music coming over the high walls of the compound as he opened the narrow gate and walked through. Inside there were six bungalow villas that encircled a large kidney-shaped swimming pool, which in turn was surrounded by plenty of grass that extended to the villa porches.

"Milton!" Jacks called from behind a large picnic table covered in meats of all shapes and sizes. Milton could just about make him out through the smoke.

He placed down an extended fork and licked his fingers before shaking Milton's hand.

"Glad you could make it. We're in for a hell of day," he said.

Jacks was playing the part of the perfect host. He was wearing a bright yellow Hawaii shirt and was ensuring everyone had a beer in their hand and had placed an order for food.

"We've got steaks, hot dogs, burgers, prawns, baked potatoes. It's the smorgasbord of all smorgasbords. What do you fancy?" He turned to Milton who was in awe by what he could see.

"You sure know how to throw a party, Carson," said Milton as two bikini-laden beauties walked past and jumped into the pool. "Beer's fine, Carson."

"I just like to call it a gathering of beautiful people. It's the Middle East's version of MTV's *The Grind*," replied Jacks as he cracked open a beer and handed it to Milton.

"Make yourself at home, John. That's my pad over there. Living either side of me are Chalky and Stardust and the others belong to Lenny, JT and Kirk. It's quite a neighbourhood eh?"

That had to be the understatement of the year. Not only did these guys work and socialise together, they also lived in their own compound.

Stardust came out of the front door of his villa assisted by Pups as the two struggled with a huge bin full of ice. They parked it next to the table which acted as the bar and started throwing cans of beer into the bin.

"Milton, my ol' pal. Great to see you here," said Stardust. "My home is your home, mate. If you need anything like a toilet or a lie down - if you know what I mean - just help yourself." Then he leaned closer and whispered, "the rubbers are in the top drawer by the side of the bed."

There was indeed as fine a spread of women as there was food. Kirk was already in the pool chatting to a couple of top-heavy beauties and Pups stripped off to his trunks and jumped in to join him.

But Milton hadn't come here to party; well, at least that wasn't his prime reason. He needed to find out more about Jacks and he had to choose his moment well. He felt there must be a treasure trove of secrets hidden in that villa of his. However, he couldn't just go and snoop around. He had to be patient and wait for his chance.

The party gathered pace under the blistering sun as the beers flowed and the food gradually disappeared. There were over 100 people there at its peak, many of whom Milton had never seen before, but they were all well aware of who Jacks was.

Jacks had the women drooling over him and the men wanting to be seen in his company. He had seen this scenario before during his first encounter in the Carter's Bar. Jacks played everyone off perfectly and was slapping high fives with anyone who offered the palm of a hand and he kissed more female cheeks than a newly wed.

The guy was sheer class. He could easily see how the man had commanded so much respect. During the whole time he had been in Dubai, he had not heard a bad word said against him and, should there ever be, that person would have to face the wrath of a loyal militia.

Towards late afternoon, Milton saw Jacks walk into his villa so he grabbed his chance. He left it a couple of minutes before walking through the same front door and calling out with a drunken slur, "Stardust, are you here?"

Jacks came into the hallway sporting a change of clothes.

"Sorry, John boy, you've got the wrong house. Come in anyway."

Milton gladly accepted and walked through the hallway and into the living area. Inside there was a huge television flanked by speakers. Modern art pictures adorned the walls and the furniture was jet black leather.

In the corner of the room there was what looked like a shrine.

"Cracking place this, Carson," Milton said as he walked towards the corner.

"Not bad at all, mate. Beer?"

Milton accepted and caught a can thrown from the door by Jacks.

Milton meandered towards the corner of the room and could make out a dozen or so pictures of Carson in military uniform: some of him in desert terrain, some as part of a group and some in various other landscapes.

"The military is what brought me here in the first place, John. If it weren't for the military I would probably be working in some shop or factory back in the UK."

Milton caught sight of a couple of medals, probably from tours of duty, before Jacks placed an arm on his shoulder and ushered him away from the corner.

"There are a dozen beautiful women out there and you are in here looking at my army pictures. C'mon, John, let's go and rejoin the party."

Milton agreed and they walked back outside into the dimming late afternoon sunshine.

The party was indeed in full swing but Milton was unable to get in the mood. He talked to girls and joined in the swimming pool games just to keep his cover, but he had other things on his mind now. He knew that Jacks had moved him away from that corner of his house quickly for a reason. Somewhere among that pile of memorabilia was the story of Carson Jacks and Milton knew he had to get back in there somehow.

Chapter 18

The mood at work was different. The focus was no longer on the job but the special duties after work. The France game was a little over two weeks away and the preparations started in earnest that day.

It was to be a week at work that no other company in the world would put its employees through: five hours of honest graft and then three hours of fitness training, combat training and finally intelligence and job execution in the classroom. Most companies' idea of group bonding would be a game of pass-the-parcel at a pathetic staff retreat.

Jacks and Chalky had cased the city well. Chalky had gone with Jacks on this occasion because, like Jacks, he had a grasp of the French language and they had returned with aerial video surveillance, maps, A to Z road maps, just about anything required to carry out a raid on a city.

Milton feared that Paris had not been targeted like this since the Second World War.

Twenty men were selected for the job; luckily for Milton it was the 12.00 to 5.00 afternoon shift of which he was a part. The morning shift, consisting of men he had hardly got to know, had worked well on the Switzerland job and was being rested for the big onslaught on Germany the following month.

It created a friendly rivalry between the two shifts and the afternoon crew accepted that they had a big job on their hands if they were to surpass the previous month's mission carried out by their colleagues.

The workouts were becoming more intense as Pups pushed everyone towards their physical peaks. The combat training also took on a much sharper edge. Kirk and JT were concentrating on close combat and combining simple boxing techniques with karate. Basically the men were being taught a more vicious discipline of kick-boxing.

The classroom sessions became more professional and methodical. Jacks would open them up by reminding his troops why they were carrying out this mission: telling them that it was for the good of the Queen and the country; drilling into them that one day the country would be great again and men like those at Expatriatedotcom would be responsible for it. He was brainwashing each and every one of them into believing that now was not the time to promote England through hosting the World Cup in 2006, which could in turn encourage a massive influx of foreigners wanting to sponge off their great country. He commanded their full respect. He had been their guardian now for many years and the men would do anything for him.

Chalky would then take over and give detailed descriptions of the city.

As the week wore on, Milton, like all the other men, was finding out his role in this operation. He could tell the other men were in their element, but he was decidedly nervous. He wasn't sure when the perfect time would be to call in the cavalry and close the operation down. He could act now, but all these men were doing was planning an operation. He felt the local authorities would be reluctant to get involved due to Jacks's link to the sheikh and, even if they did help, the men would probably get away with a slap on the wrist.

Milton would need hard evidence and that could only come by catching the men in the act in Paris and then unveiling their operation in the aftermath. That would ensure that they would be closed down for a very long time.

On the other hand, however, Milton had become a part of the family, and as his name was mentioned more and more in the classroom briefings he was feeling wanted and had become an integral part of the team.

Ten days before the match, Jacks ordered an alcohol ban and training was stepped up another notch. Milton had never reached such a pinnacle of physical fitness in all his life.

With a week to go, London had become nervous and demanded results. The newspapers were going to town on stories that rival football gangs in England were uniting for a joint assault on Paris and predicted rivers of blood running through its streets unless the authorities clamped down.

"Sir, the chiefs are getting restless once again," said Waite, who had been in France with Milton's crack anti-hooliganism team for a week already to put the ground plans into place. Border checks had been set up and almost 1,000 banning orders had been sent out to convicted troublemakers telling them to report to their local police station every 12 hours starting two days prior to the match. *The Sun* had also set up a hotline for readers to ring in and claim a reward if wanted thugs were tracked down in the run-up.

While Jacks and his cronies numbered 25 at the most, there was an army of some 20,000 Englishmen that were going to be making their way across the channel for the match; many of them up for a rumble.

"They haven't finalised their plans for attack yet, Waite. They may not even do that until the day of the game for all I know." For the first time Milton was getting a little annoyed with Waite.

"Sir, I'm only passing on the vibes I'm getting from HQ. I am under the cosh here too, you know!"

Milton apologised. "Look, Waite, from what I can gather we are going to be split into four groups of five with a further five men working on surveillance. Where we're going to be and who we are going to be with will not be revealed until nearer the game. I just do not know right now.

"I suggest that we rendezvous on the morning of the game or the night before and somehow I will pass you the plans then."

The pair came up with the idea that Milton would write down the details of the master plan and deposit them somewhere safe for Waite to collect at a pre-determined time and place. They couldn't risk being seen together and Milton was doubtful as to whether he would be able to slip away at any time in the build-up to the game. It would be a simple drop-off and collection.

Waite would then follow Milton's instructions to the word: ensure there were enough police there early to quell the trouble as soon as it began; lock up the ringleaders; disclose the truth behind Expatriatedotcom. Then, bingo, every Englishman could look forward to a trouble-free match with Germany and FIFA would be so impressed that England would be announced as the host for the World Cup 2006. It sounded simple enough to Waite, but Milton knew he had a terrific task on his hands if he were to make it happen.

Jacks was a master planner. The four separate groups of five were called Hit Squads and Milton was put in a Hit Squad that was to be headed by the burly Lenny. This filled Milton with relief as he felt Lenny could walk through brick walls. An ex-paratrooper, Lenny had been through more scrapes than a gynaecologist's tool kit and had served with JT who was quick to recommend the man mountain to Jacks during the early days.

The five-man surveillance team, which was responsible for disabling or doctoring CCTV cameras and also monitoring the trouble from the air, was called EFTA which was short for Eyes From The Air.

Milton had established that there were a number of men with helicopter pilot licences and one of them would be in the sky with Jacks and Stardust, who were in complete control of the operation.

The instructions and the sermons from Jacks were handed out in strict, disciplined fashion. No one spoke, except to ask sensible questions, as the jigsaw for the proposed mayhem in Paris was put together.

Milton was in Hit Squad One; Kirk headed up Hit Squad Two; JT was in charge of Hit Squad Three; and Chalky was in charge of Hit Squad Four.

As the week dragged on, Milton and all the other men studied the streets of Paris until they knew every nook and cranny, every coffee shop and Eiffel Tower souvenir shop and, of course, every bus depot and train station.

This was still not enough for Milton though. He needed solid evidence and that would only come in Paris. He had to be patient.

But, just as everything was coming together, his plans were reduced to tatters.

On the final Thursday at work, the men were split into their groups for their own specialist reconnaissance training work. This meant that Milton had no idea what Hit Squad Two, Three or Four were going to be up to and he was worried.

Still, his own Hit Squad's plan was applying its final touches and he was flabbergasted by its professionalism.

Hit Squad One was to fly out to Barcelona from Dubai on the Sunday, the game being on the Tuesday night some 600 miles north in Paris. The following morning, the five men were to get suited up and fly business class from Barcelona to Paris, thus avoiding any checks from immigration officers looking for gangs of possible troublemakers. They were then to stay at the five-star Chester Hotel in the north of the city and sit tight to await further instructions from EFTA who were flying direct from Dubai to Paris first class on separate flights over the weekend.

Hit Squad One had no idea how the other Hit Squads would be arriving in Paris and vice versa. It was stunning in its simplicity. Jacks was the mastermind and Milton believed that only he and Chalky were in possession of the full plans.

The weekend flew by. Most of it was spent going back and forth on the phone to Waite and his other officers who were obviously worried. Tension was mounting.

Before he knew it, he was sitting in the Dubai Airport departure lounge with Lenny and the other members of Hit Squad One waiting to board a flight to Barcelona.

"Feeling nervous?" asked Lenny, who looked as though he had bought up half of Dubai Duty Free.

"A little. It's just strange. I feel as if I'm going to war but all I'm really doing, when you think about it, is going to a football match."

"Don't worry, John, it will seem a little strange at first but you'll be okay. You get a tremendous adrenalin rush once all the fists start flying and, believe me, we'll be tucked up in bed watching glorious French porn once the referee blows his whistle to start the match!"

Milton was stunned. "You mean we won't even be going to the game?"

"Of course not. We need to get out of any trouble areas as soon as possible and besides ... I hate the bloody game!"

The seven-hour flight to Barcelona dragged. The alcohol ban put in place by Jacks meant they couldn't even enjoy a couple of beers to pass the time away. Everyone was tense though and each mind was on the job.

The five met up for a meal in the hotel that evening and Milton established that his three other colleagues were all ex-Royal Marines who had been recruited by Jacks six years earlier to work in the royal protection unit he had set up in Dubai.

They held Jacks in high regard, a story that was becoming monotonous and yet understandable to Milton after the past few weeks.

He struggled to sleep. He was less than 48 hours away from the match, possibly 36 hours away from being in the core of any trouble, and yet he still did not have a clear-cut plan in his head.

He couldn't call Waite from his hotel room, as that would ring alarm bells the following morning when checking out. He did not feel comfortable using his mobile neither. Once they had retired to their bedrooms, he gave it an hour and sneaked to a payphone some distance from the hotel.

Waite said there had been some sporadic drunken fighting already but generally the streets of Paris were calm. The main volume of fans was expected to pour in the following day.

He told Waite that he would leave clear instructions with the concierge at the Chester Hotel by 8.00 p.m. the next evening. One thing Lenny had told him was that their operation would not start until the afternoon of the game itself.

"Carson was so happy with the way it went in Zurich that he wants to focus on the day of the game these days. Always makes better TV when the sun is out!" Lenny had said.

It would give Waite plenty of time to work out counter-plans of his own, and Milton would be back in his own house in England within a couple of days. Whether he actually wanted to or not was not the question. He had to return to normal life as he still felt his time in Dubai was nothing more than a fairy tale.

Milton was at the breakfast table earlier than the others. He hadn't slept well but he was under far too much pressure to worry about tiredness.

All five were suited up and all they were instructed to carry was a change of clothing, which should be concealed in businessman-type carry-on luggage.

They would be flying back with a stopover in Barcelona, so they left any non-necessary baggage back in the hotel. Milton was hopeful that his next flight would be onward to London with a solved case under his belt.

It was the first time that Milton had flown business class and he swore it would not be his last. It was as if he had opened his living room door and sat in his easy chair, got off it an hour later to walk out of the same door and yet it was a different location.

The five smartly dressed thirty-somethings strolled through arrivals at Charles de Gaul Airport. There was an air of anticipation in the airport. Hundreds of Englishmen, many already tanked up with a bellyful of ale consumed en route, were being stopped and searched by police. Some were arguing, but everywhere they went in the airport they could hear the same chant of "ENGERLAND, ENGERLAND, ENGERLAND".

Some were singing the English soccer anthem of "No surrender to the IRA" while many others just quietly joined queues, eager to get through and into the cool Parisian air with as little grief as possible. Agitated police dogs looked rabid as they strained towards anyone stepping out of line. Drunk supporters tanked up on Dutch courage were doing their best to wind up the dogs as their handlers struggled to keep them under control.

The local police were suited and booted ready for trouble. All were well aware of what could unfold in the coming hours. After less than 30 minutes in town, Milton concluded that Paris was on the edge. A small match could ignite a volcano and everyone seemed up for it.

Lenny led the way as the five fast-tracked through passport control and were met by an airport pick-up. Forty-five minutes later they were checking into the plush Chester Hotel, just in time for lunch.

"So what next, Lenny?" Milton asked as they gathered their briefcases and walked to the lifts.

"Just sit tight in your room, order up a little room service and watch TV. EFTA will be in touch soon and we will receive our instructions on how we are to proceed."

Milton felt helpless. The day before a match was usually his most manic day. And yet here he was, tucking into a burger and fries and watching an episode of *Friends* on television.

He could not contact Waite. They had decided, as before, that mobile phones were too risky given the level of communications expertise within

Jacks's ranks. He could not even go for a walk. He had to sit tight and await further instructions. He had got this far; he did not want to cock it up now. He was frustrated. He was also in fear of the unknown.

Five hours passed before Lenny called up and told him to come to his room. It was now 5.00 p.m. and only three hours before Waite would collect his instructions.

The others arrived at Lenny's door at the same time, excited like eager kids on Christmas morning.

Lenny was staying in a suite that had a seating area and a large table on which a map of Paris had been unfurled. In his hand were two pieces of paper, which looked as if they had been faxed through.

"I've just picked these up from EFTA," he said, waving the papers at shoulder height. "We're in business, fellas."

Lenny started to read out the instructions from the paper, cross-referencing with the map.

EFTA, who had been operating in the city for two days already, had targeted the main area where the English fans appeared to be congregating which was also frequented by the French.

He drew a big black circle around the red-light area. It was well known to Milton. He had studied this city solid for two weeks now and knew every building and street in the location.

"Okay, fellas, here's the story," Lenny continued. "We leave here at 1200 hours tomorrow and it will take us roughly an hour to reach the red-light district. We will then scatter for 15 minutes on arrival and head to this pub here."

He drew a black circle on the map.

"The Dublin Arms. One of the biggest pubs in the vicinity and expected to be packed to the rafters tomorrow. Grab a drink and we will then meet up in this section of the pub at 1330 hours."

He placed the other piece of faxed paper on the table on top of the map and drew a cross on it.

Milton looked closer and could see it was a hand-drawn plan of the pub.

"As you will see, this is a pool playing area, but EFTA informs me that the table will be out of the way tomorrow to make room for more people. We are expecting around 500 to 700 Englishmen to be drinking in and around that pub. Is everyone still with me?"

The four nodded and mumbled.

"Okay." Lenny crumpled up the pub's plan and threw it in the metal bin at the side of the coffee table.

"Moving on." His focus again switched back to the map.

"This area here is around 800 yards away from the Dublin Arms and is popular with tourists and locals alike, but tomorrow you can expect it to be packed with anything up to 2,000 Froggies.

"EFTA tells me that some of Hit Squad Four will be among them, wearing French colours and will get things moving from there. Where the other two Hit Squads will be I don't know at this time, but I think it is safe to say that at around 1400 hours tomorrow they will be doing the same as us."

"And what's that?" asked one of the men.

"Ushering as many drunken England fans into that area as possible for scenes of complete and utter mayhem."

Lenny went on to explain that they would be standing close to the door of the Dublin Arms. One of Hit Squad Four would run past the pub at exactly 1400 hours wearing a blue French shirt and throw something, probably a bottle, through a window close to them.

The Hit Squad Four member would then taunt the drinkers from a safe distance and Hit Squad One's job would be to raise the anger levels among the drinkers and take off after the runner with as many of the men from the pub as possible.

They would follow the runner, or bait as Lenny called it, through to the area where the 2,000 French fans would be drinking. Two members of Hit Squad Four would be the first to clash with Hit Squad One and hopefully the snowball would roll from there. The two Hit Squads would basically grapple and generally play fight while the real stuff broke out all around them.

At the same time, Hit Squad Four bait would also have hit the pubs to which Hit Squad Two and Hit Squad Three had been assigned and they would all be converging on the same area at around the same time, just after 1400 hours.

The result would be hundreds, if not thousands, of men going toe to toe and it would take hours for the police to regain control, by which time the media would have had a field day with the coverage obtained

The plan was dazzling in its simplicity. EFTA, the surveillance team, would be monitoring the trouble from a helicopter in the sky and all the Hit Squad leaders would be linked up to them through communication devices in their ears to ensure that they all retreated down safe routes and away from police control.

Milton presumed that the CCTV cameras in the area would be doctored in a similar way to those in Zurich. By the time the news television cameras were rolling and the photographers were clicking, they would be long gone, leaving the ongoing trouble to the thugs and fighters who would inevitably be arrested and be of no use to the authorities whatsoever.

It was a plan of brilliance and Milton could understand now why Jacks had evaded him for so long, but not this time. It was six o'clock and Milton had two hours to put it into writing and leave it with the concierge for Waite's pick-up.

He was confident that the end was now in sight.

Chapter 19

Milton awoke with a start. His sleep had been interrupted all night but at some point he had slipped off and he wasn't sure whether it was the sound of a breakfast trolley being pushed down the corridor or the sunlight beaming through a crack in the curtains that woke him up.

Either way, it wasn't the wake-up call he had expected.

In his note to Waite he had ordered his right-hand man to call him at the hotel at 8.00 a.m. Milton looked at his watch and saw it was almost 9.30 a.m. Something was wrong.

He opened his briefcase, took out his casuals and rushed out of the door, still pulling the jumper down over his shoulders. He was only on the second floor so he hurried past the lifts, burst through the fire door and made his way down the stairs to reception, taking the steps two at a time.

He scurried through the lobby, past the reception and over to the concierge.

"Bonjour," said the bellboy.

"Yes, hello. I left a letter here to be collected last night and I was wondering if it was still here."

The bellboy checked the register and showed Milton that the letter had been signed for at 8.05 p.m. the previous evening. Printed next to the signature was a French-looking name. Milton didn't even bother to note it, acknowledged the bellboy and turned to dash back towards the staircase.

He turned and crashed straight into what seemed like a tree trunk.

"Steady on, Milton, what's the rush?" said Lenny, who was walking out of the restaurant located next to the concierge desk.

"Sorry, Lenny, I overslept and was just playing hell with these clowns for not giving me an alarm call," replied Milton, who was visibly shocked.

"You've missed breakfast, mate. Not to worry though, it was just a few slices of dried bread. No wonder these buggers were useless during the war. What sort of a start to the day is that?

"Anyway, mate, we'll all meet back at my room at 1100 hours to go over everything one last time. That gives you an hour or so to sort yourself out."

Milton was almost compromised. He had come close a few times in Dubai but this was the nearest yet. His story seemed to have been accepted once again though.

"No worries, Lenny. I'll get myself sorted and I'll see you there."

Milton decided to climb the stairs again rather than wait for the lift. On reaching his room, he grabbed a handful of coins from his bedside table and headed straight back out again.

He had the number for Waite's control office and called it from the same telephone box he had used the previous day.

"Why the hell didn't you call me this morning, Waite?" he said, trying not to raise his voice.

"Sir?"

"My note. I told you to call me this morning at eight."

"Sir, I didn't receive your note."

"WHAT?" This time his voice aroused the attention of several passers-by.

"Sir, we sent a car over to pick it up but it had problems on the way back."

"I do not bloody believe this, Waite!" Milton was enraged.

"A fight broke out in the city between a bunch of drunken English fans and the French overreacted. They called on every officer in the region to respond and the car on its way back from the Chester Hotel was one of them.

"There were about fifty of them fighting amongst themselves and in the middle of it a couple of police cars got torched, including the one with your note.

"I was stuck in the surveillance centre supervising CCTV coverage and didn't find out about it until midnight."

Milton could not believe it. Everything he did by himself had gone so smoothly, but as soon as something left his control it cocked up.

"I can't believe you are telling me this, Waite. Did you not think about contacting me as soon as you found out?"

"Well, sir, to be honest it was very late and everyone was heading home for the night so there was nothing much that could have been done anyway."

Milton was furious and Mount Etna was getting ready to erupt inside him. But shouting would achieve nothing and it still wasn't too late to act.

Milton told Waite to install a sizeable plain-clothed presence in the Dublin Arms pub and the area where the French fans were drinking. He then explained the plan he had been briefed on the day before and told Waite to ensure that the CCTV cameras were up and working in the areas where the clashes were expected to take place.

He trudged back to the hotel, still fuming over the incompetence of his colleague.

He made it to Lenny's room at 1100 hours and went over the plans with a fine toothcomb once more with the rest of his team.

Obviously his strain was starting to show.

"You sure you're okay?" Lenny enquired as he started to burn the maps in the metal bin.

"Yeah thanks, no worries Lenny. Just a bit of a dodgy belly. Must be all of that dry bread!"

"You're not going to shit yourself this afternoon now are you? It won't look good going into battle with the brown stuff running down your legs."

The others laughed. Milton just shrugged.

"I'll be all right, mate. Don't you worry about me. It's just first-time nerves."

The time had come. The time for one of London's leading police officers to support the start of World War III in Paris. The irony was not lost on Milton as he sped down the stairs with the men he would be sharing the trenches with. Waite had better not fuck up, he thought.

The five men jumped on a bus close to the hotel, which took them to the subway station. They climbed on board the train which was busy with football traffic dressed in blue, all of them heading to capture the atmosphere of the big match in the city centre.

Milton mused that these men, women and children of all ages would stay well clear if they really knew what was in store for them. Men and women wore their blue scarves with pride while children were decked out head to toe in their country's colours. Milton and his men were the only ones on the bus 'colourless', preferring Burberry, Stone Island and Aquascutum to Nike.

They reached their predetermined bus stop and splintered. It was easier to remain inconspicuous as individuals until they reached their assembly point. It was now almost 1300 hours and Milton did a bit of window shopping. The red-light district was a paradise for England football fans, with the neon lights prominent despite it being the middle of the day.

He popped in and out of a couple of sex shops before checking his watch and walking to the Dublin Arms. It wasn't difficult to spot. Union Jacks and St George's flag crosses were hanging out of its windows and the chants were already bellowing from the beer-bellied choir outside. The pubs hadn't shut all night and most of the lads Milton jostled past on his way to the bar had been on the pop since breakfast. He spotted a couple of lads in plain clothes that he knew from the force and did not dare to acknowledge them as he walked past. They had spotted him too and wisely avoided eye contact.

It took Milton some time to be served, but there were still a couple of minutes until he met the others in the prearranged area of the pub, which had indeed removed its pool tables to make room for the hundreds of England fans who were rapidly emptying its stocks of booze.

Milton picked up on snippets of conversation. One burly man in his forties, barely able to finish a sentence off without adding an F-word, said to his mate, "I wonder when it's going to kick off. I am gagging for it, mate. I hate the Frogs."

His mate agreed, as did several other strangers within ear shot who had picked up on the last part of the sentence.

These were the foot soldiers that Milton had seen time and time again over the last year or so. They were the ones who ended up in the cells while the generals, namely Jacks and his men, were living the life of luxury and planning their next raid.

He spotted one of his Hit Squad colleagues in the prearranged area and walked over to join him.

"Shame we haven't got longer here. I just found a cracking peep show down the road and the bird had a Union Jack tattooed on her boob," he said in a strong northern accent.

Milton shared his own experiences of the sex shops, which sounded almost boring in comparison. Still, they agreed they had achieved plenty in the 20 minutes or so that they were separated.

On the dot of 1330 hours, Lenny and then the remaining two lads arrived and everything was ticking like clockwork. The men seemed relaxed, but Milton felt as though he was ready to be sick. He hadn't been this nervous since his wedding day.

"Calm down," said Lenny. "Take some deep breaths and relax. It'll be fine."

The five chatted away and joined in a few of the football songs as the atmosphere in the pub became increasingly alcohol-fuelled.

Anti-French, anti-German and anti-IRA songs were being bellowed from the heart and it was becoming obvious that a small spark could quite easily ignite a huge fire of violence.

Milton looked at his watch every 30 seconds as it crawled closer towards 1400 hours and he still had no idea what he was going to do. He decided he would just go with the flow and try to keep his cool. He could see Lenny slip a small device into his ear and he recognised it as the same sort of communications device that he had spotted on the CCTV footage several weeks earlier back at his HQ in London; the same device that had started his trail to the Middle East and to Carson Jacks.

Lenny was taking in the orders, probably from Jacks who was circling somewhere above them in the helicopter.

"Okay, lads, everything is going to plan. I make it four minutes before show time," he said.

Milton's stomach was doing somersaults. He wanted to go to the toilet but knew he would never get back in time.

"Hey mate, don't I know you?" A well-built Scouser in his early twenties put his arm around Milton.

He was in trouble.

"Sorry mate, I don't think so," said Milton, who recognised the man as one of those he had interrogated a couple of months earlier at a previous match.

"I'm sure I've seen you at a match before. Was it when we kicked arse in Spain?"

It was indeed Spain, but the only arse Milton kicked was the man who now had his arm around him trying to remember who he was. He had been arrested for fighting inside the ground. Milton had grilled him for an hour at least. Shit.

"Look mate, you've got me mixed up with someone else," insisted Milton, who shook his head in the direction of the others.

Lenny butted in, "Sorry mate, this lad's a virgin. It's his first time away with England. As the man said, you've got him mixed up with someone else."

Lenny's imposing figure ensured that the Scouser retreated back to his group from where he continued to convince his mates that he knew Milton from somewhere.

It was a close shave and Milton wished the action would kick off soon or the Scouser with the short memory might suddenly remember who he was and that would be that.

Suddenly a window to the right of where Hit Squad One was standing caved in with an almighty crash and the pub erupted in rage.

Lenny nodded to the others. "It's time to rock and roll."

Being close to the door, they were able to leave the pub before it bottlenecked. About fifty yards down the street and wearing a French football shirt was Pups. He was shouting "Vive la France" and gesturing to the angry masses with arms wide open to come and get him. Those already drinking outside of the pub were shouting obscenities back at him and the atmosphere turned from one of general mischievousness to very tense indeed.

The plan was working.

Lenny burst to the front to lead the shouts in Pups's direction. He was one of the biggest men in the pub and most of the others saw him as a giant they could fall in line behind. He slowly walked up the street followed first by a dozen, then 20, and then well over 200 as the three other members of Hit Squad One started shouting and encouraging others to charge. Milton stayed close to Lenny.

A beer glass was thrown which Pups dodged with ease. Then one English fan, who was walking down the street behind Pups, saw his chance to become a national hero and attacked him from behind.

Pups was surprised but dispatched the man to the ground with ease. This only succeeded in inciting more hatred from within the mob who saw one of their own downed so easily by the enemy.

The shout went up to charge and the mob, which had now swelled to well over 300, launched itself down the street, knocking everything and anything out of the way.

Shop windows were smashed; bystanders were thrown to the ground and kicked as the tidal wave of terror gathered momentum. They were yelling like cavalry on horseback as their legs carried them through the streets after Pups who could have easily outrun them, but he was holding back so he remained in their view.

Their superior fitness ensured that all five members of Hit Squad One were well ahead of the others and Milton was getting caught up in the hysteria, unsure if he was shouting through fear or anger. Adrenalin opened his veins and his heart pumped double time.

After zigzagging through several streets, Lenny, who despite his size was faster than any of them, turned one final corner to be confronted by a sea of blue, out of which emerged Chalky, Pups and another man Milton recognised from Expatriatedotcom.

Lenny jumped into them followed by two others from his Hit Squad and they went crashing over some tables that were outside a coffee shop.

Within a split second, the rest of the English herd had caught up and mayhem broke loose.

There were hundreds of men fighting as the two sides clashed. The French were shocked but easily outnumbered the English fans who were fighting as though their lives depended on it.

Milton became involved in a scuffle with a young Frenchman no older than 18 who was taking wild swings at him. Milton merely restrained him and tossed him into the path of oncoming English boots and fists that were ploughing through the area.

He observed as Lenny waded his fists through one Frenchman after another, and by now the three members of Hit Squad Four that 'greeted' them had thrown off their French colours and fled the scene. Their job was done.

As the fighting continued, it looked as if the English were getting overrun and then another mass roar could be heard as hundreds more Englishmen arrived on the scene from another direction. Milton could see JT close to the front and he was also flooring one Frenchman after another. The scene was a battleground. Milton was just trying to avoid punches and was wondering where the hell the police were. He could see the odd one or two trying to break up scuffles but was expecting hundreds to be arriving on the scene. Overhead he could see the helicopter from where Jacks and Stardust would be planning the Hit Squads' getaway routes.

It was getting messy. One Frenchman in front of him was being kicked time and time again by a group of Englishmen. It sickened Milton. He had to do something. After all, he was still a copper at the end of the day.

He intervened and told the men to move onto someone else.

"C'mon lads, this one's had enough," he shouted as he pulled the hungry pack of wolves from its lifeless pray.

"He's still breathing ain't he," replied one.

Then Milton was stunned to see that one of the lads administering the beating was the Scouser from the pub moments earlier.

Amidst all the pandemonium, his memory was jogged.

"Wait a minute," he said, grabbing hold of Milton's shirt. "You're that pig who gave me a hard time in Spain."

He launched a right-handed haymaker at Milton, which caught him beneath the eye, ripping open the skin with the gold sovereign ring on his index finger. Milton stumbled but managed to stay on his feet and broke free from his grip.

Before a second punch could be thrown, there was another huge roar of a hundred voices as a third marauding group of England fans poured into the street. This must have been Kirk's bunch.

Milton knew he had to silence the Scouser and so strung together a flurry of punches into his face and held on to his jumper as he fell to the ground.

"You fuckin' pig," he shouted as he crashed to the ground, blood pouring from his mouth.

Milton was in a crazed adrenalin rush and continued to kick the Scouser as he tried to get to his feet. The man was down and out and Milton moved on as swiftly as possible.

His was a small part of the massive picture being painted in that street but he had to move quickly. After all, he had just laid out a man wearing an England shirt.

He looked for Lenny, who was close by throwing Frenchmen around like rag dolls. Lenny put his hand to his ear as more instructions from EFTA arrived.

"Milton, head for Prince's Street and down to Seventh Street Station. See you in the Gents," he shouted down Milton's ear from close range.

He signalled the same to the others and they quickly dispersed.

Milton legged it as fast as he could. He was breathing heavily now and felt knackered.

He took a left off Prince's Street and into Seventh. He knew the route well from the maps and figured he had about another 300 yards to the station.

He was soon there and he ran into the public toilets, moving straight to the basins to catch his breath. He was the first there and tried to take in everything that had just happened.

That was the worst fighting he had witnessed yet and he had been slap bang in the middle of it. He leaned over the basin and looked to the floor, wondering where the hell the police were.

The floor started to change colour. It was turning to red. He looked up to the mirror to see that the cut under his eye was leaking badly. It needed stitching up.

The others soon joined Milton. Lenny was the last to arrive.

"I love my job," Lenny declared with barely a scratch on him. His knuckles were covered in red.

The others had cuts and bruises but were in ecstasy too.

"Better than any roller-coaster ride; better than a bungee jump; better than sex!" said one as he slid his back down the wall to rest his bottom on the floor.

In the distance they could hear sirens as hundreds of police were directed to the trouble.

"That looks pretty nasty," Lenny said as he moved Milton's hand away from the cut.

"What am I going to do?" asked Milton, fearing he would be left behind on the battlefield.

"Don't worry. We just sit tight here and wait for EFTA. You see they are not just our guides from the air, they are our Florence Nightingale too!"

With that, a man came running into the toilets. Milton recognised him as one the lads from Expatriatedotcom.

"Someone call for an ambulance?" he said. It seemed this was a predetermined meet with the 'doctor' making his scheduled house call.

"Milton seems to be the worst. Just patch him up, Wilko, and we will all get the hell out of here," instructed Lenny, who walked to the entrance to ensure that no one came in. Another of the lads walked up to the street to act as a lookout. The other men helped themselves to the medical supplies carried by Wilko in a small backpack.

"Looks like you'll need stitches," Wilko said as he opened and closed Milton's cut with his thumb and index finger.

He pulled out a small box from the backpack which he opened by the sink they were standing at.

"Sorry, Milton, no anaesthetic so this is going to hurt a tad."

Wilko delicately threaded a piece of material through the eye of a needle and guided it towards the gaping wound just under Milton's left eye.

"Steady, Wilko, I don't want to lose an eye," said Milton, who was still high on adrenalin.

"Don't worry, mate, I've done this a thousand times ... just never on a human."

Wilko punctured the skin with the pin beneath the cut and began weaving up and down, criss-crossing the wound. It reminded Milton of the *Rambo* film when Sylvester Stallone patched himself up after almost severing his arm.

He was in unbearable agony, and felt the warmth of blood pouring down his face.

After less than a minute, Wilko declared, "There we go. Come back and see me in a week's time. In the meantime, no booze, no sex and no fighting!"

The whole side of Milton's face was tingling with pain. His Aquascutum jumper was covered in blood but one of the lads returned with a souvenir t-shirt he had picked up from a tourist store outside. He unfolded it and it read: 'I love Paris'. Instead of the word 'love' there was a heart and the writing was in different colours. Milton popped it on as they left the toilets, despite the ridiculing from his colleagues, and they hopped on the next train that took them out of the city.

It was now 1500 hours, an hour after the trouble had started and the men were on their way out of the city. Job done.

Smash and grab, hit and run, whichever term was to be used, it was a mission executed with military-style precision; and, without a doubt, successful.

Apart from curious glances on the train from suspicious passengers, Hit Squad One were returning to the hotel undetected and the following morning they would be flying back to Barcelona, and then on to Dubai.

Milton didn't have a clue what had gone wrong. He didn't know either what had happened to the other Hit Squads, but he did know that he had just been a part of one of the biggest single incidents of soccer hooliganism that the world had ever seen.

Chapter 20

"Get yourselves cleaned up and we'll watch the matinee show back in my room at 1630 hours," said Lenny when they arrived back at the Chester Hotel. "And bring your own beer and popcorn because you're not having any of mine."

That gave Milton about 15 minutes to himself. Wilko had done an excellent job on the cut. It looked like six stitches in the mirror's reflection but it could have been more.

He quickly showered and washed away all the dried blood. He took a cold can of pop from the minibar and placed it against his face, which was still burning with the pain.

It was a soothing relief, but before he had a chance to do anything else his phone rang. It was Lenny asking what was taking him so long.

"On my way, Lenny," said Milton as he grabbed a couple of beers from the minibar, slipped the hotel bathrobe over his boxer shorts and t-shirt and headed out.

The four were glued to the television in Lenny's room like kids watching cartoons. Lenny and one of the men were sitting in the two chairs with the other two on the floor. They couldn't even prise their eyes away from the television to acknowledge Milton as he walked in.

Milton sat on the edge of the bed and watched the television in horror. It was like a morbid throwback to the time he was sitting alone in his hotel room in Zurich watching pictures of all the trouble that had gone on that afternoon.

It was classic déjà vu: same channel - CNN; same woman reporter; same television pictures that were being beamed across the world - only this time they looked worse.

The female American accent could hardly get the words out fast enough:

"Police have made dozens of arrests, mainly England fans, who appear to have launched an organised attack on this street. At two o'clock this afternoon, many men, women and children were making the most of a mild autumn afternoon. It's a street also popular with tourists with its coffee shops and traditional Parisian architecture.

"Then terror struck as between 500 and 1,000 English supporters - and I use the term loosely - wreaked havoc and turned this beautiful area into a battlefield."

The camera moved its focus from the woman reporter to the scenes over her shoulder. One shopkeeper was sweeping up broken glass that probably used to fill the gaping hole that was now exposing his shop to the outside world.

There were waiters turning tables back upright and medical workers and police attending to the many injured that were still scattered across the street.

"Authorities say that 57 people have been taken to hospital, several of whom are reported to have suffered stab wounds and many have fractures. Witnesses report scenes of utter carnage and I am joined now by Richard Lecroix, who was drinking at one of the coffee shops in the area.

"What happened here Richard?"

The microphone was thrust in front of a pale-faced middle-aged man who had scrapes on his forehead. His blue French rugby shirt was torn around the collar and he looked as if he had been in the thick of it.

The man spoke in an Anglo-French accent.

"It was terrible. Very frightening," he said, shaking his head. "I was drinking with friends and then suddenly, boom."

His hands moved in a way suggesting a bomb had gone off.

"All these shouting men came from everywhere and started kicking and punching anything in their way. I saw one lady get punched. As I helped her from the floor, I was kicked in the head and just lay on the floor, praying they would leave me alone. I have never been so scared in my life."

The Frenchman started weeping. He was heavily traumatised.

"What's he crying for? He's back on his feet ain't he?" Lenny joked.

The footage from the afternoon's events was then repeated.

A male anchorman in the studio with a deep American accent narrated.

"Here we see it again, the scenes of absolute chaos as hundreds, possibly up to 2,000, football followers clashed in one of the most popular areas of Paris. This of course is a huge blow to England's hopes of hosting the World Cup finals in 2006. That decision, as we said earlier, will be made in a couple of months by FIFA and pictures like this will not have done them any favours."

Milton watched in horror as the pictures showed hand-to-hand combat on the scale he had not witnessed at any football match before. This action took place long after the Hit Squads had evacuated. Not even the television cameras would have been in the area that got hit awaiting potential trouble.

"Shame we left so early," said Lenny. "All this was going on well after we were there. At least TV caught the tail end of it."

The narrator said it was some 30 more minutes before calm was restored and police were rounding up scores of England fans they suspected of being involved.

"They haven't got a clue," said one of the men sitting on the floor. "We're here, hello." He waved at the television.

"Well," declared Lenny. "Here's to another highly successful job done."

Lenny stood up and raised his beer and the others rose to their feet and copied. Milton reluctantly joined them.

He stayed with them for about an hour but the pain from the side of his face was becoming unbearable. He was not in the mood for socialising so he made his excuses and retired to his room.

It had been the failure of all failures for him.

If his instructions had been followed, all the carnage he had watched on the television would have been avoided. Arrests would have been made and Expatriatedotcom would have been smashed. He could have gone home.

Instead, the situation was worse now than ever and his pride was hurting more than the cut on his face. It had been a shambles and this time he was convinced that he would be the scapegoat; both barrels of the gun wedged in his mouth with the trigger cocked.

He spent the evening lying on his bed trying to think of excuses but the pictures on the television still shocked him despite his being in the thick of it and seeing it first hand.

What must his superiors be thinking?

But something wasn't right in his own mind.

He had at one point during the afternoon enjoyed the rush. Charging through the streets and the original hit were one of the most adrenalin-fuelled moments he had ever experienced.

He then became scared when the Scouser spotted him but he almost enjoyed punching him to the ground and kicking him in the middle of the mass brawl.

He could not understand himself at all anymore. Had he gone too far? Whose side had he just been on?

Should he just leave the hotel and return back to the UK before it got out of hand? His gut feeling told him to go, but his cover was still intact and the cut under his eye would ensure a hero's welcome back in Dubai.

He was too tired to make decisions as he lay on the bed. Despite all the physical training he had gone through, he was exhausted and decided to leave any major decision making until the morning.

For now he had a football match to watch on the television.

* * *

Twenty-four hours later Milton was back in the Pheasant Hotel in Dubai. The staff, who had come to like their permanent visitor, were concerned to see him with a cut under his eye. Gopal had brought painkillers to his room, which did the trick, and by the time Milton arrived at Expatriatedotcom on the Thursday morning he was feeling a lot better.

As he walked into the warehouse, he was greeted by cheers from the morning shift which had watched the action on television. He was getting pats on the back and his hand shaken by just about everyone as he walked to the staff room. He felt a weird sense of pride and adulation.

"John Milton, you are my idol," said Stardust, who was already in the staff room. "Straight in there with the first wave and Lenny said you did one hell of a job. Let me shake your hand."

Milton smiled but flinched; it still aggravated the cut.

"Wilko patched you up pretty good," Stardust said as he inspected the damage. "You're lucky he came to your Hit Squad. Some of the other medical guys would have used knitting needles and wool to fix that cut."

He laughed and ruffled Milton's hair.

On the way home from Paris via Barcelona, Milton had decided he would continue to keep his cover. He couldn't face the dishonour of returning to London in failure anyway. Instead he had returned to the sort of hero's welcome that he had never experienced in all his time in the force.

"How did it look from the chopper?" asked Milton.

"Chaotic and bloody marvellous!" replied Stardust. I was gagging to put the chopper down somewhere to join in but couldn't. It was hard up there. Police were coming in from every avenue and up Prince's Street was about the only way out. We sent the other Hit Squads out that way too."

"Is everyone okay?" enquired Milton, who was genuinely concerned.

"Every single one. You were about the worst injured, John. You need to sharpen up, my friend!"

Now he could see why he had become so frustrated since he started with the anti-hooliganism squad.

They were like ghosts, in and out before the Old Bill arrived. All the police would be left with were the men who had followed like sheep; untrained, unfit, drunk, and easy to arrest.

No wonder they had got nowhere over the previous 12 months. The latest figures from Paris showed that 400 England fans had been arrested. Again those 400 were like the thousands they had arrested already across Europe at the other matches. And for every 100 arrested and later banned from travelling, there were always going to be another 100 to pick up the baton for the next match. In some strange way, as with terrorism and suicide bombers, the television images of football violence made it appealing to a whole new audience at home itching to get involved.

The facts were simple and clearer to Milton than ever before. Stop Jacks and you stop the mass trouble. For sure there would be fights, but nowhere near the scale of the past few matches.

Almost 200 people had been treated in hospital; thankfully there had been no deaths. For that, Milton was hugely relieved.

As he finished his tea, ready to start his shift, the warehouse erupted in cheers that could only mean one thing: Jacks had entered.

Through the glass door he could see the lads mobbing Jacks and a couple hoisted him onto their shoulders. They were chanting "Carson, Carson" and he was like a World Cup winner waving down to them with a huge grin on his face.

This had been the most successful operation so far for the group and Jacks was a happy man.

"Lads, to celebrate the past week's success, there will be another party over at ours this Saturday and we're closed Sunday so we can party all night!"

This news was greeted by celebratory cheers as Jacks was gently dropped to the ground and Milton could only watch in awe. He had probably become Jacks's greatest admirer, which made him even more determined than ever to bring him to his knees.

Chapter 21

Saturday soon came around and once again the party was in full swing by early afternoon. This time Jacks had hired an acoustic band that was playing some chilled-out background music by the pool.

Everyone was in celebratory mode. Most people were well and truly tanked up already and Milton saw something that almost made him sick.

Chalky was bent over stark naked and Stardust was pouring a jug of beer down through the crack of his backside. Underneath was young Pups trying to drink as much of the beer as possible. Most of it was being spilled all over his face but he didn't care. He was the centre of attention and loved it. He was also the only person daft enough to carry out such a hideous act! The crowd chanted "Down, down, down" and Pups stayed there until the jug was empty.

Pups emerged, fists clenched in the air and everyone was cheering. It looked as if the mother of all parties was taking shape.

Milton was spotted and the crowds swarmed around him to find out about his heroics a few days earlier in the Paris mayhem. Word had spread quickly and, despite his initial concerns, Milton took to his new-found iconic status. His years in the Met had never delivered this sort of adoration from his colleagues and he wallowed in it.

He explained how he had wrestled with countless Frenchmen and how one had got a lucky punch in. He easily won over his audience. He was a hero now just like the rest of them and very much part of the furniture.

It was in stark contrast to the rest of the day he had endured.

Twenty-four hours earlier he had read the riot act to Waite, who had been through plenty of drama himself.

Waite had informed Milton that the French authorities had been obstructive all week in the build-up to the match. The French felt they were able to handle the situation better than anyone else and were unwilling to co-operate with their English counterparts, particularly on the day of the game itself. Waite and his team were powerless and completely undermined by their French counterparts.

Luckily for Waite and Milton, the lack of co-operation went all the way to the top and the seniors had become well and truly pissed off with the French too. Subsequently a war of words had broken out in the aftermath with the British blaming the French for everything that went wrong. The under-fire British Government used this as a damage limitation exercise in what was a grim situation. But, simply put, in the eyes of the world the English thugs had won the day.

Sir Michael had actually gone on television to say that the French had ignored the warnings from British intelligence. He dropped short of explaining what that intelligence actually was to protect Milton, which only drew even more ridicule from across the English Channel.

"Our men have risked their lives trying to pre-empt the trouble but our intelligence information fell on deaf ears," he had said.

Waite said that the French had considered the area where the trouble kicked off as low risk and they had expected more trouble in other parts of the city. Apparently, the French only had 16 officers on duty there at the time. Waite had just as many British officers in the area in plain clothes. At the height of the trouble, the police estimated that over 1,000 men were fighting.

It was shocking news. Milton could not believe how incompetent the French authorities could be. During his time with the squad, he had come across know-it-alls in most countries but had generally found them helpful come match day.

He always got the 'this is our country and this is how we do things around here' attitude but he was an excellent negotiator and would always talk them around in the end. Massaging egos and kissing arse were his key tactics. In fact it had become his only method of communication with these people.

The French, in contrast, were more stubborn and they had paid a heavy price. Maybe if he had been in control instead of Waite things might have been different, but it seemed that he was in the clear as the mud continued to fly between Paris and London.

In fact his conference call to HQ that very morning started with Sir Michael apologising to Milton.

"We realise you were badly let down and we can only be thankful that you are still in one piece and your cover has not been compromised," he said.

Milton had got what he wanted. He was told just to keep his nose clean and await further instructions.

The good news was that Waite had ensured the CCTV footage was intact and he was to spend the weekend with his colleagues analysing it frame by frame.

Milton had experienced a week at work to remember - or forget - and it was time to unwind. Right now he was in exactly the best place to do both. He accepted a bottle of beer handed to him by one of his 'groupies' and took a well-deserved swig.

"If someone deserves a beer more than anyone else, it's our much respected, much loved new recruit, John Milton," Stardust declared as he filled the funnel of beer once again and motioned with his finger for Milton to come towards him.

Once Milton had the freshly opened bottle taken from him, Stardust helped him into a chair with his spare hand and moved the tip of the funnel towards Milton's mouth.

The cheers howled out as Milton braced himself for two pints of ale to reach his kidneys in about ten seconds flat.

Stardust removed his palm from the bottom of the pipe that was connected to the funnel and ale gushed into Milton's mouth with tremendous force. He lost his senses for a split second but opened his eyes to see a hysterical crowd shouting and Stardust jumping up and down.

"Heeeeeero, heeeeeeero, heeeeeeero!" Stardust led the chants and helped Milton to his feet.

"Wow!" said Milton, as he let out a seismic belch that could have registered on the Richter scale.

"We slipped in a couple of vodkas too just to help you get in the swing of things!" declared Stardust.

It had an immediate effect. He was soon dancing, drinking more beers and then dancing and drinking more beers. Song merged into song as drinking game merged into drinking game. Conversations were replaced by indiscriminate shouting as the sun retreated unnoticed behind the Arabian Gulf.

The next thing he knew he awoke on a couch. He couldn't remember where he was but it was familiar.

He lifted his head from the cushion and saw that it was morning and he was still fully clothed. Someone was passed out on the floor to the side of him and the creaking sound he made as he moved was a sign that he was lying on leather - black leather in fact, and he soon realised that he was crashed out in Jacks's front room.

His initial loss of bearings was quickly replaced by a thumping headache as a woodpecker behind his left eye tried its best to tap its way out. He felt like shit.

But then a burst of sudden reality ensured that his thumping headache was soon forgotten. He lifted himself off the chair and gingerly stepped over the parallel body on the floor as if walking on eggshells.

Through the window he could see Jacks and Stardust cleaning up around the pool. JT was just sitting on a sun lounger holding his head and Kirk was floating fully clothed on an inflatable armchair in the middle of the pool. He had probably been there all night. The clock on the wall showed it was approaching 10.00 a.m.

Milton had an opportunity to return to the corner of the room that Jacks was quick to usher him away from a few weeks earlier. He checked that his colleagues were still occupied and, with the coast clear, he moved closer.

The desert pictures looked as if they had been taken during the Gulf War. He recognised a younger Stardust in one of them. His hair was closely cropped and his face looked sunlashed.

The other pictures also looked as if they had been taken during his days of service. There was one picture of him posing in front of a giant Irish tricolour flag painted down the side of a house wall. Over it was written: "Death to the British Army"; an obvious photographic memento from time served in Northern Ireland.

Another showed him posing, again in British army colours, with what looked like Asian, probably Malaysian, soldiers. The setting seemed jungle-like.

The range of pictures confirmed to Milton that Jacks had done time in the Special Forces. There was no question in his mind about that now.

Nothing seemed out of place. The pictures proudly reflected a career that many other men had also endured. But it did not explain why his name had not shown up on any of the checks that his team had conducted with the Ministry of Defence. There was no record of Carson Jacks ever serving. It was a mystery.

Then Milton noticed a chain draped over the corner of one of the pictures. Its pendant was hidden by the frame. He reached his hand around the back and felt immediately that they were dog tags. He pulled them into view and got the breakthrough he was looking for.

Looking back at him from the shiny rectangular piece of steel was the name Jackie Carson, Royal Signals, complete with rank and number.

"Jackpot," Milton had whispered to himself.

Suddenly he heard someone coming through the front door and could hear

Stardust and Jacks chatting. A split second before they entered the front room Milton just managed to jump back onto the couch.

"Morning, sleeping beauty," said Jacks, prodding Milton in the tummy. "It's mid-morning, John, and time to get yourself home so we can tidy this place up."

Milton pretended to be stirring and slowly opened his eyes.

"I feel like shit!" he exclaimed.

The front room had beer bottles lying everywhere which meant that the party must have moved indoors at some point. Milton could not remember; he was plastered the night before.

A taxi arrived soon after and he ordered the driver to take him back to the hotel as quickly as possible. Now he could eventually find out who Carson Jacks really was.

* * *

"That's Jackie Carson, Waite, Jackie Carson." Waite seemed strangely subdued on the other end of the line. "He served with the Royal Signals up until 1990. Get the Ministry to run it through the computer."

Waite still seemed quiet. "Okay sir, will do," he said.

"Well don't sound so bloody enthusiastic about it, Waite." He could sense something was up. "What's happened?"

Waite took his time to reply, and cleared his throat with a sharp cough.

"Sir, we were going through the footage last night to get clear photos for *The Sun* to publish and we came across a very interesting, yet vicious, character who looks to be new to the hooligan scene."

"Just ignore it, Waite. We've got everyone we need to nail over here."

"That's what I mean, sir."

"What?" Milton was perplexed.

"You see, sir; that person, sir, is you, sir."

"What are you talking about, Waite? You've been working too hard; you need a holiday."

"No, sir, it's as clear as day. The camera picked you up kicking the shit out of some bloke. That bloke, sir, is still in hospital in Paris with a broken jaw."

Milton took his time to reply. That damned mouthy Scouser had come back to haunt him once again.

"Who knows about this, Waite?"

"Just the gang in the office, sir. Only us. We were pretty shocked when we saw it."

There was another short silence as both men wondered what to say next. And then Waite shocked his boss with a stunning question that they were all desperate to ask.

"Are you still on our side, sir?"

"For God's sake, Waite, of course I am. I interrogated that bloke at the Spanish game. He recognised me, Waite. It could have blown the whole operation. I had to shut him up somehow or my life would have been in danger. He was just some pissed-up idiot. He could have closed us all down."

"It looked brutal, sir. Are you sure you're okay?"

Waite fished for words of reassurance and Milton sensed the question was aimed at his mental state of mind rather than his physical health.

"I am fine. Tell *The Sun* that the CCTV hasn't helped us at all on this occasion, and you have got to shut that Scouser up somehow. He must not report this to the French or I am in the shit. We are all in the shit."

Milton could tell that Waite was worried. After everything he had been through, it would be the easy option for Milton to switch sides. He could remain in Dubai and not have to worry about his shambolic private life in the UK anymore. He could pick up big bucks working for Jacks and basically enjoy himself.

But he was still confident of cracking this case. All those years in the police force had made him a determined man.

His loyalty was questioned during his undercover drugs days. He felt he never did get the credit he deserved from that. This was going to be different and he had become more determined than ever to crush Jacks.

He did not care about England's bid for the World Cup any longer. Neither did he care too much about his career anymore. And as for his marriage? That had not crossed his mind in days. He just wanted to get this over and done with and the only way he could do that was by bringing these men to book; the men he had become a brother to over the past few weeks. He really had become a part of their family.

Chapter 22

Back in London, Waite reassured the team that Milton was still firmly with them.

The CCTV footage had provided excellent coverage of what had happened in that Parisian square, but their joy at landing firm evidence had turned sour when they saw that their chief appeared to be one of the main perpetrators. It had been a stunning revelation that they had refused to accept on the face of it.

Waite had addressed them all and explained the incidents building up to the moment when Milton was caught on camera beating the Scouser up. The troops were both satisfied and relieved. Milton owed his junior a drink.

"Our focus now is to turn to a Jackie Carson," he said. "Detective Inspector Milton has reason to believe that this is the correct name for Carson Jacks, which is an alias. Run it through all the usual channels and I want answers within three hours. Come on, let's move."

The reaction of the staff proved that their minds were back on the job after a difficult past couple of days as they dispersed to their workstations.

Various snippets of information filtered back to Waite over the next couple of hours but he asked his excited team to save their findings for the briefing, which commenced three hours later on the dot.

The buzz of chatter as he entered the briefing room showed Waite that they had the required results.

"Okay, who's first?" he said.

Sergeant Sandra Bennett couldn't wait to share her news. Her job had been to run his name through the Ministry of Defence's army personnel records.

"Jackie Carson, it appears, was an exemplary soldier." She was reading her notes obtained from a conversation with a Ministry of Defence bookworm.

"He joined the Royal Signals at 16. He was selected for training to the communications division of the Special Air Services at 20, making him one of their youngest members ever. But for some reason he was kicked out 18 months later. He was dismissed from the Regiment."

"Do we know why?" asked Waite.

"No, sir, the military are very cagey about this one, but they have promised to let me have something by the afternoon."

"To be honest, Waite, that is nothing that I didn't really suspect already," Milton said down the phone minutes after the briefing finished.

Waite was a little disappointed. He was eager to inform his boss of his findings and called him immediately after the briefing. But he still had more information to share.

"We've also tracked down his mother," he added.

"You beauty, Waite. That's more like it. Where is she?"

"She is 67, widowed, and living in Watford. We're heading up there this afternoon to see her."

"Just make sure you take Sergeant Bennett with you to give it a woman's touch."

Waite knocked on the door of the semi-detached house, which was located in a well-kept suburb of Watford. There was no answer.

"Hello? Mrs Carson?" Bennett called out.

"She's around the back," shouted a white-haired lady from an upstairs window of the house next door.

Waite and Bennett opened a waist-high garden gate at the front of the house and walked alongside the garage to the back garden. Mrs Carson was making the most of the last gasps of decent weather before the onset of winter blues.

She was kneeling on a cushion with clippers in hand trimming a plant.

"Hello, Mrs Carson?" Bennett called out again.

"Oh, hello." Mrs Carson seemed shocked at being addressed by a uniformed officer. "Just making the most of this lovely weather."

"I don't blame you," said Waite, who would rather have been sitting in the beer garden of a pub himself.

"I'm Sergeant Waite and this is my colleague Sergeant Bennett." They produced their identification. "We'd like to ask you a few questions about your son."

Mrs Carson's face turned to an expression of sadness.

"You had better come inside then," she said in a soft voice. "Please, come this way."

She led her guests through a narrow back door which entered into the kitchen. Once inside, she put the kettle on and invited Waite and Bennett to sit in the immaculately kept living room. One of its main pictures on the wall was a head shot of Jacks wearing military attire. He looked no older than a teenager.

"It was the proudest day of my life when that photograph was taken," she said, seeing the two were looking at the picture. "It was taken down in Aldershot and my Jackie had just passed out from his basic training and into the main regiment. He was so happy."

"So tell us about your son," Waite probed.

"Why all the interest after all this time?" she asked.

Bennett took over. "Ma'am , we have reason to believe that your son may be involved in criminal activity."

"No way, not my Jackie. It's impossible. He couldn't do such a thing."

"I'm sorry, Mrs Carson, but we have evidence to the contrary," said Waite.

"No, it's impossible. You see my Jackie was killed nine years ago in the Gulf War."

The news stunned Waite and Bennett who were now completely baffled. Milton had not shared all of his information with his junior officers for fear of his story sounding too far-fetched. He had simply told them that Jacks had been on a mission in Kuwait during the Gulf War. He had shared with them nothing on the fallout from their operation.

"He went on a special assignment just before the main air bombardment, to save an Arab sheikh or something, but he never made it out."

"Who informed you of his death, Mrs Carson?" asked Waite, who was not convinced.

"It was one of his colleagues that was on the mission with him. He said the Ministry would not confirm this because he was on a top-secret mission working for an Arab family. It was the saddest day of my life. Losing a husband is bad enough, but a son? Well, you always expect them to be here long after you go."

Mrs Carson went on to describe her son's upbringing. His father was a communications engineer and had taught his son the trade since he could walk, spending hours together in the shed at the back of the house.

"His father died in a car accident when he was 14 and it changed his life," she said.

"He was one of the brightest lads in his school, but he had made his mind up that he wanted to dedicate his life to what his father had taught him. The only way he believed he could do that was by joining the Royal Signals.

"I tried to keep him in school. He left with 10 O levels you know. But his mind was made up; Jackie was stubborn like that, just like his father.

"The stuff he was taught during his first couple of years in the army his father had already taught him and the army soon realised that they were dealing with a communications expert who was only 18. He was even teaching the teachers at times.

"He came home a year or two later and said that he had been selected to apply for the SAS. That was the last time I saw him until he left the forces."

"And why did he leave the army?" asked a softly spoken Bennett.

"He never did say. But what I can tell you is that he was never the same man again. My son may have died during the Gulf War but I felt I had lost my son the day he left the army."

She may not physically have had a body to bury but emotionally her son was already six-feet under.

Waite was convinced that Jacks was indeed Jackie Carson. During his phone call later that afternoon with Milton, they decided that he obviously wanted his mother to believe that he was dead in order to sever completely his ties with the UK, substantiating the story Pups had told Milton a few weeks earlier.

But the most compelling news came later that afternoon when the Ministry contacted Bennett again.

"Sir, you are not going to believe this," Waite said to Milton.

"Jackie Carson was kicked out of the military for football hooliganism."

"You are right, Waite, I do not believe you!"

The story was to send shivers down Milton's spine.

"Sir, Jackie Carson, or Carson Jacks as you now know him, was stationed in Turkey in 1990 when England played there in a friendly before the World Cup finals.

"There was a lot of trouble. Thousands of England fans had travelled out for a bit of winter sun and there was also a large garrison of British troops stationed there as tension was rising in neighbouring Iraq.

"Jacks was there with the 22nd Squadron of the SAS, a specialist tactical division used to monitor the movements of Northern Iraqi forces by intercepting their radio transmissions.

"Anyway, he was off duty and in Istanbul on the day of the game and apparently got caught up in the trouble. But wait for this …"

Waite took a deep breath. He was talking at 100 mph, but tried to steady himself.

"The Ministry sent over CCTV footage of a couple of incidents that were used as evidence during his closed-door trial. In fact this is still a Top Secret file.

"The first showed him fighting inside a pub which was completely wrecked by the trouble. You can clearly see him using his professional fighting techniques."

"So was he jailed as well?" Milton interrupted.

"No, sir. Once he was found by the Turkish police, they checked his ID, saw that he was military and handed him over to the British military police to deal with. The court took into account what had happened to him after the fight and he was simply discharged from the regiment."

"What do you mean, 'found' and 'took into account what happened after the fight'?" Milton was curious.

"Take a deep breath, sir. This is where it gets nasty.

"It appears that the English fans were hugely outnumbered at the pub and were overrun by the Turks. Most of them legged it, including Jacks, but he became isolated from the others. He ran down a narrow alley pursued by a mob but it was a dead end. CCTV footage from a nightclub that has a staff entrance in that alley picked it up."

"What did it show, Waite?"

He could hear Waite swallow with a gulp before he continued.

"Sir, Jacks was heavily outnumbered. From the footage it looks as though there were about eight of them. They just overwhelmed him but he put up a fight. He kept getting up but they just kept beating him and beating him time and time again. It was brutal, sir.

"Eventually he didn't get up and lay motionless on the floor. Sir, the dirty bastards raped him while gloating and cheering. Absolutely filthy animals."

Waite was battling to relive the horror of what he had just witnessed on the television screen.

"He was defenceless. He was raped by three of the men and I could tell he was still just about conscious as he was still moving his arms and trying to push them away.

"There was nothing he could do, sir. The others just stood there laughing and I'm sure they would all have raped him but something happened and they fled. A minute or two later the police arrived.

"He spent two weeks in hospital with a fractured skull and several fractured ribs. He was dismissed by a military court several weeks later."

There was a deadly silence. Milton was stunned and felt as though the wind had been kicked out of him.

He could not believe that a man so revered and respected by so many had suffered such a degrading and disgusting act.

"Are you sure it's Jacks?" he asked.

"Absolutely. His face matches all the pictures you have sent through. I am 100 per cent certain that Carson Jacks and Jackie Carson are the same man. 100 per cent."

Milton felt sick. He had not seen the footage but Waite's graphic description painted the macabre picture in his mind.

It was no wonder Jacks had fallen out of love with his country. He had been through one of the most inhumane episodes possible for any man or woman and all his country could do was say he was no longer fit to defend its borders.

It would be enough to push many over the edge.

Not only did Jacks now have an army at his own personal disposal, he also had a motive for revenge. It was getting messy but Milton was convinced that he was the only other person at Expatriatedotcom to know the real story of Carson Jacks and he decided that was the way it would remain.

Chapter 23

Three weeks to go. Three weeks before the two biggest rival countries in modern history went to war on a battlefield once again ... only this time the battlefield was to be a football pitch.

While the result of the match between Germany and England was as meaningless as the Christmas Day no-man's-land kick-about between the two countries during the First World War, the stakes had never been so high since the two clashed in the World Cup final in 1966.

FIFA had narrowed their shortlist of bidding countries to host the World Cup in 2006 to these two. Their decision was coincidently expected within the weeks after the match and the winner would secure a windfall of billions of pounds ploughed into its economy.

While the bid organising committees' campaigns focused on the benefits that such a tournament would bring to their countries, the media had concentrated their coverage on the story that everyone wanted to read and watch.

Football officials, politicians, even the Prime Minister and Chancellor, were all roped into the debate as counter-accusation followed accusation that each other's nation was incapable of hosting such an event.

The football hooliganism problems plaguing England's national team had cast a huge shadow of doubt over its bid and the Germans were slight favourites to land the biggest show on earth.

Of course, if England fans ran amok in Germany in three weeks time, as they had done on their previous trips abroad over the last 14 months, then the coffin lid would be firmly nailed down and England's bid would surely be buried once and for all.

Milton was again reminded of this during his latest conference call with his hierarchy. They had come out of the French trouble relatively unscathed, with the French authorities carrying most of the responsibility due to their unwillingness to co-operate.

Word had also got through to Jacks and he was fuming. The sole intention of his ruthless campaign was to position the nation as a white, Christian country unable to control its spiralling undercurrent of thugs and show that England was not a place for foreigners anymore.

"It appears, men, that we wasted our time in France," he said at a classroom session. "France was a write-off. We'll go all guns blazing into Germany and finish this job off once and for all."

He was concocting a plan that would involve all the men at Expatriatedotcom, which meant some 50 trained fighters - specialist football hooligans.

Life for Milton at Expatriatedotcom was never going to be the same. On the one hand, he truly admired Jacks for bouncing back from such a terrible experience all those years ago. But, on the other hand, he was fearful of what he may be capable of.

Jacks was calling the German match 'the Big Bang' and said it was time to gain revenge for the torture that country had put their fathers and grandfathers through during the two world wars. The men were being whipped up into a frenzy at each session and Milton knew they would be like a crazed pack of wolves by the time they reached Munich.

In the meantime, back home Waite was enjoying a better relationship with the German police than he had experienced with the French force and everything seemed to be running to plan.

However, one thing did not add up for Milton, who was continually fighting his inner self over theory after theory. With no one alongside him to bounce ideas and scenarios off, he was playing his own devil's advocate.

Since the France game, Jacks had made two trips to Germany alone and Interpol transport records showed that he had flown to Berlin, not to Munich where the match was being played.

He also recalled that Jacks had made two 'business' trips to Berlin in the weeks running up to the France game. Munich was some distance from Berlin. There was no point planning trouble there because Jacks would not have the backup of his thousands of foot soldiers who inadvertently played a huge part in his successful missions.

Neither would there be the TV and newspaper entourage in Berlin. Without them, his operations were a waste of time and effort. The unwitting propaganda juggernaut carried his anti-everything-not-English message to the world.

He could not be flying to Berlin for a connection on to Munich because it was easier to fly direct to Munich from Dubai.

Things weren't adding up.

He had to find out why Jacks was flying to Berlin and what he was doing there. The excuse that he was there for work did not stick anymore. His opportunity would come during the week before the game was to be played.

Milton found out through Stardust that he, Jacks, Chalky and JT would be flying to Munich as the initial intelligence gatherers. Stardust let it slip that Jacks would be flying to Berlin first to tie up a few business loose ends and would catch them up in Munich the following day.

Milton had become convinced that Jacks had an ulterior motive to his football hooliganism operation and was sure that the answers lay in Berlin.

He could not go himself - that would be far too risky - so he put his trust in Waite, who booked a flight to arrive in Berlin the day before Jacks was expected to descend.

Such was Milton's fear about a breach of security that he and Waite were the only two to know about this plan. Waite simply told the team that he was taking a couple of days off to be with his sick mother.

Waite was to trail Jacks's every move from when he stepped foot off the plane in Berlin to the time he left.

"I want you close enough to smell his aftershave," said Milton. "But stay out of sight. This man is a master at communications remember, but we have surprise on our side. He will never suspect that he is being followed, I am sure of that. If you are compromised, Waite, your life will be in danger. Just be careful."

* * *

Although Waite had never actually seen Jacks in the flesh, Milton had supplied plenty of pictures. The image of Jacks as a teenager on his mother's wall and the grainy CCTV images from his barbaric attack were also still fresh in his mind.

Most of the new pictures were from the barbecues held at Jacks's villa, but they were good enough for Waite to recognise him immediately as he came through the arrivals gate at Berlin.

Waite trailed him like a customs officer through to the pavement outside the arrivals hall, where he was surprised to see him climb into a waiting limousine with darkened windows. The uniformed driver welcomed him with a salute and opened the door to allow him into the back seat.

Hmmm, Waite frowned to himself. What are you up to?

Waite summoned the next passing taxi and trailed the black car through the busy streets.

They followed the limo for almost an hour until it pulled up at an official-looking building which had the German flag proudly flying over its entrance. It looked like a civic building of some sort.

Jacks got out and was welcomed at the foot of the building's steps by two suited middle-aged men who warmly shook his hand and led him indoors.

Waite paid the taxi driver and walked to a small coffee shop across the street. From its window he could monitor the front door of the building.

"One tea, please," he said, placing his order before the approaching waiter had time to speak. "That building across the road is very impressive. What is it?"

The waiter finished writing Waite's order down on his small pad.

"Ah, sir, I have had the pleasure of looking at that magnificent building from this window for 14 years. It is the pride of Germany," said the waiter, who appeared to be reminiscing about past times.

"Yes, indeed," said Waite. "But what does it house? What is inside?" He gestured with his hands to make the importance of his question clearer.

"It is the Ministry for Local Affairs. I think you would call it in England the Home Office?"

What the hell would Jacks be doing at the Home Office in Germany? Waite felt very uncomfortable.

The hours passed and Waite was struggling to keep his eyes open. Surveillance just wasn't his field and the waiter's grasp of English wasn't quite good enough to talk about anything other than football and that damned building across the street.

"I remember once when your Maggie Thatcher came here," he said whilst cleaning the table next to Waite. "Whatever happened to Maggie Thatcher?"

By now, he was well and truly bored and was willing to talk about anything.

"She's now a page three girl," he joked, knowing full well that his new-found friend had no idea what that meant.

The waiter simply appreciated the information.

Waite, in his boredom, imagined that during the course of the next week that same waiter would be saying to an Englishman sitting in the café, "I remember once when Maggie Thatcher came here. She's working as a page three girl now you know."

Four hours had gone by and the light outside was fading fast. Not too dark for Waite to see the building opposite, though.

Finally Jacks emerged from the building side by side with a man who had become well known to Waite, and to just about everyone else who owned a television set in the Western world.

"Hans Schmidt," he said to himself in disbelief, but the waiter heard him.

"That is right, sir. Hans Schmidt," he repeated.

Schmidt was a German MP appointed two years earlier to head up his country's bid for hosting the World Cup 2006. He was a national iconic figure and had been on television dozens of times over the past weeks pushing Germany's bid and berating the English effort.

He garnered the sort of respect from the people of Germany that Jacks enjoyed in his own small world in Dubai. Schmidt was climbing the political ladder fast and a successful bid for the World Cup was expected to lead him to the country's top job, that of Chancellor. Time and time again he had gloated to the world's media about how England was unable to control its hooligan problem, and yet here he was, laughing and joking with the biggest exponent of the English disease.

The penny dropped. Jacks and the Germans shared the same ideals and goals. Both wanted England portrayed as a far right nation allergic to foreigners. Jacks's reason was to exact revenge on a country that had disowned him during his time of need; the Germans' to ensure they won the right to host the world's biggest event of any kind.

"I do not believe this," said Waite as he clambered out of the café for a closer look.

The two spent a little time exchanging jokes next to the open door of the limo before embracing and going their separate ways - Jacks into the limo and Schmidt back into the building.

Waite had seen enough. The light was too dull to get pictures, so he ran as fast as his legs could carry him to the nearest phone box and frantically tapped in Milton's number at the hotel.

Milton had deliberately taken the day off sick - citing the pain of his facial wound - so that he could wait by the phone.

"Sir, we have opened a can of worms here now," said Waite.

He went on to tell Milton the lot.

"Hans Schmidt!" was all Milton could muster.

"Yes, sir. Jacks must be collaborating with the Germans. He has been festering after the way he was treated all those years ago and now he is about to unleash one hell of a revenge."

"Hans bloody Schmidt?" Milton was still struggling to accept it.

"What do we do now, sir?" asked Waite.

Milton rested the phone to his side as he gathered his thoughts. He had to find proof linking Jacks to Schmidt. There was only Waite's word so far linking the two. In hindsight he wished he had assigned a full surveillance team, but not in his wildest dreams did he expect to uncover such a twist in Berlin.

He had honestly suspected that maybe it was a business trip to Berlin. Maybe Jacks had a woman there? Maybe he was meeting fellow hooligans? Never in a million years did he suspect that Jacks would be meeting a Minister.

He had to find out what they were up to. In court, they could quite easily say that they were inking a deal to buy 10,000 German flags from Expatriatedotcom.

In reality, though, Milton was sure that they were inking a deal to unleash terror on the streets of Munich a week later.

Of course, it was all starting to make sense. Riots on the streets of Germany initiated by the English would virtually guarantee FIFA giving Germany the nod. However, if Milton could piece together the jigsaw in court and reveal that Germany was actually working with a rogue band of English hooligans to instigate the trouble, that would surely rule them out of the equation and England would be victorious in its bid.

Milton told Waite to return back to base immediately to co-ordinate the operation on the ground and he would be in touch. He cautioned him not say a word about this to anyone else just yet.

It left him pondering in his hotel room.

Why would Jacks want to become an ally of the Germans if he was so patriotic?

Why?

Then it dawned on him.

All that stuff in the classroom about patriotism, about helping England to be great again, was bullshit. He had brainwashed his men into believing that they were on some crusade to put the 'Great' back into Britain when all the time he was betraying his country.

It was now becoming clearer why Jacks was making his journeys to Berlin alone. If Stardust, Chalky, or any one of the men really knew what he was up to, he was sure they would lynch him.

Then he remembered the other thing that Jacks kept close to his chest - the company accounts.

Milton had never been able to understand how the business could pay such high wages to so many men without going bankrupt. Of course, there must be a source of money coming from elsewhere and that source must surely be the Germans.

However, it was all circumstantial evidence and nothing that could stand up in court. He needed hard evidence: a paper trail; or, more importantly, a money trail.

It was obvious now to Milton that the beating and the rape had stirred up a deep hatred and feeling of betrayal towards England and this was his way of exacting revenge.

The incident in Turkey was followed by his own regiment, which had in some respects become his family, kicking him out. The mission to free the Arab sheikh was dismissed by the British Government and that must have pushed him over the edge. Ensuring that his mother thought he was dead meant he had no reason to return to the country that had turned its back on him. He had been biding his time for revenge.

He had patiently recruited his own followers, who had unwittingly been used as pawns in his determined bid to make England pay for what it had done to him.

Germany was to be his swansong and he had to be stopped - and what a swansong he was planning.

Chapter 24

The intelligence unit returned from Munich with the usual confidence. The men had less than a week to go. The physical and combat training had reached new levels and the classroom sessions were becoming more precise.

Once again, there were to be four Hit Squads. This time each one would have ten men instead of the usual five.

"I am expecting double the impact this time. Munich will be the epicentre of the earthquake and the aftershocks will shake the rest of Germany," Jacks said in one of his speeches, which were becoming more Hitleresque as the game approached.

Milton was once again assigned to Lenny in Hit Squad One, together with the same three men that had comprised his team in France. Five others, who missed out in France but were full of what they had achieved in Zurich, were also assigned.

It was to be a carbon copy of what had happened in Paris weeks earlier: four Hit Squads, each with their own travel itinerary and each with their own trail of destruction, and all leading towards a central battlefield. All four Hit Squads would lead the England fans to a predetermined area of Munich in which the maximum carnage could be achieved.

Milton was desperate. He needed evidence and believed the bank records would provide it.

He waited until Jacks and the other members of Eyes From The Air had departed, two days before the Hit Squads, to make his move.

It was Sunday and he was due to fly out on the following afternoon. The match on this occasion was to take place on the Wednesday evening.

He left the warehouse with the rest of his shift shortly after 8.00 p.m. He jumped into his taxi, but ordered it to stop just around the corner until everyone else had cleared the building.

Expatriatedotcom hired a local security company to watch the building, which consisted of four Indian guards who were paid a pittance in wages. This meant that the building was not fitted with alarms. After all, Dubai enjoyed a virtually crime-free environment.

He had left a window narrowly ajar in the staff room and sneaked to the back of the building to climb in. The staff room was close to Jacks's office where he was sure the records must be kept.

He wriggled through and stretched a leg to the floor, then let his body weight fall on the one leg before pulling his back leg through.

He could see a couple of the guards chatting at the far side of the warehouse. He knew a third would be at the front gate and the other manning reception, which gave him a clear passage to Jacks's office.

The lock required his best burglary skills to open and he was in. He carried with him a pen torch because the light in Jacks's dreary office wasn't the best.

Keeping out of sight, he crept over to the filing cabinet, which, to his surprise, was unlocked. Jacks was so confident of his status that he probably didn't think anyone would dare to go through his records. After all, he was never late with their hefty pay cheques, so they didn't have any reason to question him.

He flicked through the folders inside the top drawer. It was immaculately organised. There was a file for each worker, but there was no sign of one labelled 'Finance'.

Working his way down the cabinet, he finally opened the bottom drawer and found exactly what he was looking for.

Inside were the complete accounts for the company. These included the order books, purchasing books, client details and, at the back and almost concealed in a separate area, bank statements.

Milton removed the file and laid it on the floor in front of him. He pulled out a bank statement dated three days earlier, which showed a payment made to the company of 15 million dirhams, which converted into almost three million pounds. The direct debit had been made by a German bank.

He looked back through some of the previous statements and discovered that, in a period of three months alone, almost seven million pounds had been paid in direct debits from the same German bank.

The Germans were funding Jacks's operation. He looked back further and saw that the transactions stretched back as far as 18 months, around the same time that the main outbreaks of hooliganism had started and not long before he had set up his unit.

He folded the latest bank statement into his pocket and placed the file back in the cabinet. He retraced his earlier route into the building and was back out and into the waiting taxi within minutes.

Milton was on the phone to his superiors as soon as he reached the Pheasant Hotel. Even if the evidence were enough, which it wasn't, he did not know where Jacks or half of his men were. Some were already operating in Munich and others were on their way.

The agreed plan of action with his stunned superiors was for Milton to proceed in the same way as he had done in France. He would wait to hear the feedback from the advance surveillance team and their plans and then relay these to Waite who would act accordingly.

Air traffic over the city on the day of the game would be monitored and helicopters suspected of carrying Jacks and the surveillance team would be grounded soon after the trouble was thwarted to ensure that they would not be able to provide getaway avenues for the Hit Squads.

It was going to be a gamble: they were going to let the trouble brew and then choke it immediately.

"Catch the buggers red-handed," as Sir Michael had said.

The revelations had shocked Sir Michael, but they knew that the next 48 hours were going to make or break their careers.

* * *

Milton was back at Dubai Airport departures lounge again. It seemed like only yesterday that he was preparing for the France game.

This time they were flying to Innsbruck in neighbouring Austria and then hiring cars for the journey across the border and on to Munich. They were to fly back direct to Dubai from Munich, but Milton was confident this time that he would be flying direct to London.

The evening in Innsbruck consisted of more bragging from his colleagues in Hit Squad One and they set off early the next morning to Munich.

They hired three cars and left at different times, but all arrived at the Stanin Hotel before lunch. The operation was ticking like clockwork once again.

Milton checked in with Waite, who was not staying that far away himself. Waite informed him that some 12,000 England fans were expected, not to mention the thousands of off-duty British soldiers who were also stationed in Germany.

About 50 arrests had been made already, mainly as a result of drunken brawls, but that was merely child's play compared with what was expected to be unleashed on the day of the game in 24 hours' time.

"Right lads, my room at 1600 hours. I am in 515. Do not be late," Lenny had instructed.

Milton was one of the first there - eager for information; eager for the beginning of the end to start.

Chapter 25

Milton was not going to take any chances this time. He could not possibly fail. This was the last chance saloon for the whole operation. England was relying on him to come up with the goods and there was no way he was going to mess it up now.

Milton arrived in Lenny's room wired up so that every single word, every cough, could be taped and used as part of his growing portfolio of evidence. He took a seat with Lenny, who had already prepared his suite to host the mini-gathering. He had cleared a decent-sized area next to his bed so that everyone could get a close look at what was to be placed on the coffee table in the middle.

"I want you to be my Number 2 on this, Milton," Lenny said. "I'm going to need a strong deputy and I trust you more than the others."

The vote of confidence warmed Milton because it confirmed that his cover was still well and truly intact. He had wrestled with his own conscience in the week running up to the departure. These men had become his friends but he was now going to have to let go.

The men all arrived within a few minutes and were anxious to learn of their roles. They were like school kids waiting to find out about a field trip.

"So come on, Lenny, don't be shy, what's the plan?" asked one.

Lenny unzipped a leather document case and pulled out several papers. He then opened up a map of the city of Munich on the coffee table as the men gathered around. On it areas had been marked in thick black ink where their Hit Squad would first gather and then later 'engage' the enemy. It was as precise and clinical as the previous sortie, but with double the men this was going to be some finale for Jacks.

There was going to be a war on the streets of Munich on a scale never seen before in peace time and Lenny described it as glorious and implementing Jacks's vision. The men were all visibly excited as they took their notes and retreated to their individual rooms to memorise the timetable. The layout of the city was already well known to them through the classroom sessions back in Dubai. All they needed to do now was to remember where to be and at what time. It was so simple even an idiot could be a part of it, let alone trained military men.

But Jacks's confidence in his plans meant that there was never a Plan B and Milton was sure that if they could ground the chopper and cut off the Hit Squads before they reached their targets then it would be game over. He knew where his Hit Squad was going to strike, but he could only predict that the others would hit the same square at roughly the same time from different directions. All entries into that square had to be policed heavily.

"You happy with all that?" Lenny asked Milton as he crumpled the map into a ball. "It's going to be one hell of a day, so I suggest you get some rest, mate."

Milton saw his chance to seize some more vital evidence. The paperwork was always burned after the briefings, so Milton offered a hand to take the paper ball off Lenny.

To his surprise, the burly hard man handed it to him.

"When you burn it, make sure you do it on the balcony because otherwise it will set off the fire alarm," he warned. "Here, mate, take these with you too."

To his amazement, Lenny handed Milton all the paperwork before he slipped off his shoes and lay across his king-size bed.

"And shut the door will you on the way out."

Milton now had everything: the bank statements linking Expatriatedotcom to Germany; the tapes of them discussing how the raid was going to work in Munich; and now the written plans too. What he didn't have was information about where the other men would be. Munich was a huge city and they could be anywhere. They were still going to have to let the violence start and then make the arrests at the right time. It was going to be a risk but it was surely going to work.

Within an hour of the briefing, Milton met with Waite some distance from the hotel to relay everything in person to his second-in-command. There were to be no hiccups this time. Waite was in awe of his boss as he described when, where and how the raids were going to take place. He handed over all of the evidence and wished his colleague luck.

Milton's healing cut was also a war wound for Waite to admire. It was the first time that the two had seen each other for nearly two months, but they withheld the pleasantries and the general chit-chat.

"Just do not let me down, Waite," was all Milton could think of as he turned and headed back to his hotel.

Waite had 24 hours to ensure that the English police's anti-hooliganism squads could prepare themselves, and thankfully their German counterparts were well on their side too. After the fallout from the French game, they had no choice. A half-hearted German police operation would not be looked upon favourably by the footballing powers when announcing where the 2006 World Cup would be held.

Milton returned to the hotel in good time to join the others for an evening meal and then retired to his room to go through everything over and over again. He could not afford to overlook a single detail … it could not only cost him his job but also his life.

Chapter 26

Five hours to kick-off and the city centre bars and cafés were already full of football fans doing their best to drink Munich dry. Naturally the English fans were the loudest and seemed in good spirits, but the overall atmosphere in the city was as tense as it had been at the previous matches. Overweight men with tattooed forearms taunted and gestured to just about anyone and anything that wasn't English. The local Turkish population seemed to cop most of the abuse, but that was nothing compared to the odd brave - or stupid - soul that wandered past wearing anything German.

"Two World Wars and one World Cup," was their most popular chant.

Milton lit a cigarette; he had hardly noticed that he had become a smoker again. He had promised himself never to touch them again after his previous undercover job busting the drugs ring. He had been true to his word until arriving in Dubai.

This was just one of the many things that had changed about Milton without his realising over the past few weeks.

He took his position in the Irish pub across the road from where a huge throng of English fans had gathered. He sat out of view from the road but could hear the chants coming from the 200 or so voices some 30 yards away.

He made eye contact with the men from his Hit Squad, who were already in the pub, and they slowly started to assemble as the time of action - 3.00 p.m. - drew ever closer.

Milton could tell by their mannerisms that they were feeling as tense as he was. Jacks had worked his magic on each and every one of them over the years and they were determined not to let their messiah down. Lenny arrived last and the crew of ten was complete. It was Paris all over again for Milton and he was on edge. He had never been so nervous, but was doing his best not to show it.

"All right lads?" asked Lenny with a confident smile.

The general response was positive, but Milton felt like a footballer ready to take to the field before a cup final. The group chatted and melted into the general scenery of the pub, which was filling with England fans unable to get a beer in the packed bar across the street.

The men regularly looked at their watches and, as 3.00 p.m. drew nearer, they gulped down the remainder of their drinks and waited in silence. To the uninitiated, they just looked like a regular group of blokes enjoying a trip abroad. But in just a few minutes they were about to unleash hell.

Milton could feel his brow becoming damp, so he swiped his forearm across it.

"Damn, it's getting warm in here," he commented to one of his colleagues.

It fell on deaf ears. All the men wanted to hear now was the signal to allow them to kick into action.

They did not have to wait long. An explosion could be heard outside the pub and by the time the men had got outside there was a huge billow of smoke. It was the tear gas cylinder hurled by Pups, but it had failed to go through the window and instead had ignited harmlessly on the pavement outside. A huge roar came up from the mass gathering of Englishmen across the street and Pups was in trouble.

The canister was supposed to go through the window of the pub Milton was in. Thus, by the time the men across the street realised what had happened, Pups would already be on his way.

But it had not, and Pups, standing in the middle of the road between 200 angry Englishmen on one side and dozens of confused and dazed Englishmen emerging through the smoke on the other, was a sitting duck. What made it worse was that a German scarf covered his face, part of his guise as a rival supporter touting trouble.

Milton emerged through the cloud and through his watery eyes he could make out the angry pack converging on its prey. Pups was the cornered fox and he had no way of escaping the clutches of the hungry hounds that soon dispatched him to the floor with huge roars of approval from the bystanders.

Milton moved forward to try to intervene but Lenny held his arm.

"There's nowt we can do, John. Let's go," he said.

Milton felt helpless as Lenny took up the baton, realising that the plan had to continue despite Pups's demise.

"There's a load of Krauts up this street. Let's do 'em," he shouted and gestured for the rest of the army to follow.

First two, three, four, then dozens and scores of men took up Lenny's battle cry and disappeared up the street. Milton started to follow but turned back to see Pups. He lay motionless in the street as each rampaging Englishman who went past directed kicks at or stamped on his limp body.

Milton rushed over and pushed them away.

"All right, all right lads, he's had enough. There's plenty more up there. This one's had enough for one day," said Milton as he knelt beside Pups who was barely recognisable.

As the rampaging mob continued to file past, some of their spit caught Milton and few even bothered to check on Pups's condition.

"German scum" and "Kraut" were coming from the mouths of the intoxicated pack, which soon thinned out as the yobs hurried to catch up with the mob ahead, baying for German blood.

Pups was lifeless. Milton removed the scarf from his face, which was badly disfigured. He cradled him up onto his thigh and tried to bring him around. As he touched the youngster's face, he could feel that the jaw was hanging together by a thread and his nose had become a bag of skin and crushed bone fragments. His eyes were already puffed up. He had taken a bad beating but, to his horror, Milton noticed blood seeping from Pups's midriff. He tore open the buttons on his shirt and saw a gaping wound just above his belt line. He had been stabbed, maybe twice. Milton took the German scarf and tried to stem the flow of blood. He was numb as he felt the life leave Pups's body with the unstoppable flow of claret.

The medics arrived within seconds and ushered Milton away. Out of the corner of his eye, he saw a television camera crew running towards them. It was time to make himself scarce and catch up with the mob ahead.

He took one last reluctant look over his shoulder and watched the medics kneel alongside Pups, creating a hive of activity. Milton knew that it would be the last time he would ever see Pups alive.

Milton followed the path laid out by Lenny the previous day and within a few minutes he had caught up. As Lenny attempted to lead the mob into one of Munich's main squares as per the plan, they ran into a wall of riot police who were waiting for them.

Milton breathed a sigh of relief, as he knew his plan had worked. There were some 300 fans fighting a losing battle against just as many riot police and the two water cannons were sending troublemakers crashing to the floor with the power of a heavyweight champion's punch. Milton could see Lenny. He was trying to put his communications device into his ear and was looking to the skies, but there was no Eyes From The Air; no helicopter relaying a getaway route; no big brother looking after them.

Milton could see that some of the Hit Squad were already being restrained by the police and Lenny realised that the plan had been thwarted. They were in trouble.

He spotted Milton.

"We've been rumbled, Milton. We have to abort. Go and get Pups and I will see you back at the hotel," Lenny said with a firm grasp on Milton's upper arm.

Before he turned to flee, he caught sight of the blood on Milton's hands.

"Where's Pups?" he asked. His question was met by a blank expression from Milton. "Where's Pups, Milton?"

"It didn't look good, Lenny. We have lost him I think," replied Milton, who was still feeling numb.

"Lost him? You mean he has been arrested too?"

"No, Lenny. I think Pups could be dead. He had been stabbed."

At that moment, Milton felt that he had lost a friend. Pups may have been the youngest of the group and the subject of their practical and verbal jokes, but he was a good lad and Milton had grown fond of him. The nightclub trouser incident, the prostitute with the ice cream and hearing the heartfelt story of the death of his brother had all made Milton respect the kid.

"Shit. That is all we need; a man down. Look, get yourself to the nearest bogs, clean yourself up and I'll see you in two hours back at the hotel. Good luck, mate."

Lenny, dealing with the death of his comrade as if it had happened in the trenches, turned and headed off down a side alley away from the trouble.

Milton separated himself away from the fighting and found a small public toilet close by. He checked outside to make sure he wouldn't be cornered and headed straight for the washbasin. His hands and forearms were covered in Pups's blood but luckily his short-sleeved shirt was still relatively clean. Only his trousers had specks of blood from where he propped up Pups but it was certainly not enough to arouse suspicion.

Within minutes he was in the back of a taxi and on his way to the hotel. He was going against the grain of late-afternoon traffic, which predominantly comprised green and white security vans steaming into the city centre.

He knew it had been a success. Certainly Hit Squad One had failed to engage in any mass trouble with the German fans and the grounded chopper meant that they had enjoyed a further success there. The only way he would find out if the rest of the Hit Squads had been thwarted was by returning to the hotel where everyone was due to reassemble.

Milton should have been a relieved man. But seeing Pups had made him sick to the core and the fact that he was returning to the lion's den made matters worse.

He ordered the taxi to stop sharply, and on the side of the busy road he doubled up, emptying the contents of his stomach onto the pavement. Wiping his mouth, he made the decision there and then that this was it. Never again. After all, he was a human getting paid an average wage. How he had ended up in this position God only knew, but at that time it seemed that his life was in tatters. He had watched as one of his friends had been beaten senseless and the reason he couldn't do anything was because of his stupid job. Life was never going to be the same again … he hoped.

Chapter 27

Milton headed straight to his room when he arrived back at the hotel. He threw his spare clothes into his bag and, as he pulled the zip across, he noticed the light was flashing on his bedside phone. It was a message from Lenny saying he was back already and that the rest of the guys - or at least those who had not been arrested - were to meet in his room.

Milton thought about turning his back on it there and then but knew the job was not complete yet. Jacks was still a free man and he had to know where he was.

Before arriving back at the hotel, Milton had contacted Waite, who confirmed that a team of officers were on their way over.

It seemed like an eternity to Milton as he travelled in the lift up the half dozen or so floors to Lenny's suite. He did not even wait for the lift doors to open all the way, squeezing himself out and then running along the corridor to room 515.

He knocked and in an instant the door swung open sharply. It was Kirk.

"Hi Milton. Glad you made it out too," he said in his strong Northern accident.

Lenny was stripped to his boxer shorts and was cleaning himself up in the bathroom and Chalky, Stardust and JT were sitting stone-faced and deadly silent around the TV set.

"What the hell happened out there?" said Milton to no one in particular. No one answered and Milton joined them by the TV.

"Pups is dead," said Chalky without pulling his stare away from the breaking news.

The announcement had just been made that a German fan had been stabbed and had died in hospital from his injuries. His identity had not been revealed and the lads knew then that it was Pups. The men ensured that they carried no identification in case this sort of thing happened. They would rather die nameless than risk blowing the whole operation. Stardust was noting down the name of the hospital where Pups had been taken on the back of a cigarette packet. Milton couldn't work out why.

The rest of the news broadcasted the success of the police operation, which had prevented a full-scale riot in the city's main square. It said hundreds of fans had been arrested, including the ringleaders. Milton looked around the room and knew that this was far from the truth. Members of Expatriatedotcom had indeed been arrested, but certainly not the generals. They were larger than life and sitting with him in the hotel room. He just wished that Waite and the backup cavalry would arrive soon.

Hardly a word was said before the door swung open and Jacks entered the room. He was visibly upset and, judging by the scratches on his face, he had been through a scrape himself.

He grabbed a Coke from the fridge and sat on the corner of the bed. He soon replaced the TV as the centre of attention.

He described how EFTA had gone to the helicopter pick-up site and found that it was swarming with police.

"They were waiting for us. There were a lot of undercover guys there but they stuck out like sore thumbs," he explained.

They had spotted the danger and retreated. By then, though, it was too late to get within communications range, thus leaving the men stranded.

Then he concluded something that sent a shiver down Milton's spine.

"They knew we were coming so someone has stitched us up."

Milton hoped his guilt wasn't showing, otherwise his life was in danger. Kirk was standing by the bedroom door and there were five other highly trained killers in the room with him.

"You are right," said JT. "We charged towards the square and it all seemed to be going well, but there was a cordon of riot police ready and waiting for us. We were sitting ducks. They even had the trailers there ready to throw us into. Someone grassed us up, Carson."

Jacks got up from the bed to pace the room, only stopping to look at the scratches on his face as he walked past the mirror.

"It must have been someone quite high up among us. There's no way one of the boys would have sold out. Life is too sweet for them."

Milton was becoming increasingly agitated, a position not helped by Lenny who had suddenly stopped drying his face in the bathroom and was staring straight at Milton.

Jacks continued, "I thought I knew everyone at that company inside out. I thought I had gained the trust of everyone, but someone has turned on me.

"Some bastard who knew the plans relayed them all to the fuzz."

Lenny had twigged. He walked slowly out of the bathroom and never broke his laser-like gaze at Milton.

Milton was shaking his head ever so slowly. He realised that Lenny had worked it out and in some way hoped he would maintain his silence.

The burly Lenny continued where Jacks had finished. "You mean someone who could be fairly new to the set-up, Carson? Someone who perhaps was not there from the start? Someone who just turned up out of the blue to join us?"

All the men looked at Lenny and then turned to Milton as they twigged on. Milton was in trouble. Big trouble.

Lenny grabbed Milton by the throat and threw him against the wall, maintaining a tight grip on Milton's windpipe.

"Why Milton? Why have you done this?" screamed Lenny, spitting into Milton's horrified face.

"Easy, Lenny. What are you talking about? Milton couldn't have done it. He's one of us," said Stardust, realising that he was the man who had brought Milton into the fold in the first place.

"After I briefed the boys yesterday, I gave the papers to John to burn. It all makes sense now. He knew everything and has the evidence to throw the book at us. You are one dead duck, son."

Milton knew the game was up. As Lenny squeezed his windpipe tighter, he managed to wrestle himself away and fell onto the bed.

Before Lenny could launch another barrage of violence, Jacks stepped in.

"Enough, Lenny," he said.

Lenny retreated and Milton rubbed some life back into his throat.

"Why, John? Why have you sold us out?" he asked.

Milton looked up from the bed and, still rubbing his throat, spouted out the truth.

"My name is Detective Inspector John Milton of the Metropolitan Police's anti-hooliganism task force and I have been searching for you men for almost 18 months," he admitted.

You could have heard a pin drop as the men took a sucker punch straight to their stomachs, knocking the stuffing completely out of them.

They had grown to admire Milton as a friend and a comrade only to find that they had been welcoming the leader of the opposition. It would have been like Hitler's war cabinet appointing Winston Churchill to the board.

How could they have been so stupid?

Jacks could feel the rage building from within, but he spoke with a calm voice.

"You've let us down, John. Have you understood nothing about what we have been trying to do here? We have been fighting for our country's honour and future and you now tell us that you are on the other side helping to send England to the gutter? I liked you, John. I really thought we would be doing some marvellous things together, but I'm afraid you've let me down; you've let the lads down, but you've also let yourself down."

Milton heard a click as Kirk flicked the lock on the door. The men rose to their feet and circled the bed. They felt as betrayed as their leader and it was time for retribution.

Milton felt like General Custer on his last stand, but he had one last throw of the dice to escape with his life.

"If you feel so passionate about England, Carson, why have you been ruining its chances of hosting the World Cup?" he pleaded.

"You know the score, John. We don't want pictures of England going to the world in 2006. We will rise again as a powerful nation. A nation that is proud and says no to immigration, wasters, perverts, and any other growing band of losers calling it home at the moment."

Milton had to speak fast as he was running out of time.

"So if you are so proud to be English, why have you been working for the Germans, Carson? Or should I call you Jackie?"

Jacks was stunned. Stardust was the first to speak.

"What the hell are you going on about, Milton?" he said. "What is he going on about, Carson?"

The men were well and truly confused.

Milton looked Jacks in the eye as he relayed the story of Jacks's dealings with the Germans. The lack of interruption meant that his audience was listening. He even went back as far as what Jacks used to be called, but he did not go so far as to reveal the details of his ordeal in Turkey, that resulted in his dismissal from the Army.

Suddenly Jacks's world was turned upside down. He was a beaten man and he knew it.

"Tell us this is not true, Carson. Tell us we haven't been working for the fucking Krauts all this time," Chalky pleaded with his fallen idol.

Jacks looked at the men, and for the first time Milton could see an emotional weakness within. His eyes welled up as he told them the whole story of how he was dismissed from the army; the Gulf War; and then how he was approached by the Germans regarding work for his redundant army.

"I carried on for you guys. You trusted me and if the Germans hadn't come along you'd all be back in the UK standing on some nightclub door or watching out for thieves in Marks & Spencer's. The company was not making money and, admit it lads, you were all getting bored. I love you guys. We have been through so much together and I couldn't just sit by and watch you all go."

If the men were horrified to find out that Milton was an undercover policeman, they were mortified to find out their beloved boss had double-crossed them too. They were too shocked to react.

Not a word was spoken as Kirk opened the door and tilted his head downwards. Jacks turned and walked through. Milton thought he should try to make some sort of arrest, but he was still unsure of his own position. He was stuck in a hotel room with men he had come to trust and love and he felt he owed them something in return.

"In the next few minutes, this place is going to be crawling with police. If you leave now, I will give you free passage and this incident never took place."

It was not a tough decision for the men to make.

First Kirk, then Stardust and Chalky, then Lenny and finally JT filed out of the room and the heavy footsteps outside told Milton that each one beat a hasty retreat as soon as they entered the corridor.

Milton breathed a huge sigh of relief and lay back on the bed. He was absolutely drained. It was kind of over and yet it wasn't.

Jacks's army had been smashed, but at the same time he and his disciples were gone; they had disappeared into the darkness once more. But he was sure this time he was not going to see any of them again. Certainly not at a football match anyway.

Chapter 28

The Dubai police arrived at Expatriatedotcom's warehouse the next day to carry out a raid, but they were too late. It seemed that Jacks did have a contingency plan after all and the place had been burned to the ground. The police suspected arson but showed a reluctance to investigate it further. Maybe this was a parting gift from his royal partner. There was no way he was going to get back to the Middle East now. All airports were on full alert and so one last phone call to a friendly ear had sorted out the destruction of any evidence of his existence left in Dubai.

He was probably in Germany, but Milton knew he could be just about anywhere.

In the 24 hours since the match, England's World Cup bidders proclaimed to have smashed the hooliganism ring while Germany's bidders were praising their own police operation for thwarting mass violence instigated by the English. Gold stars all round.

Milton's evidence was digested by his bosses, but without the ringleaders in jail they had little to celebrate. The bank statement was not evidence enough to prove the German link - the payments could relate to legitimate business transactions, he was told. And spouting off a story that a trained English cell based in the Middle East was funded by the Germans to wreak havoc on European football matches would be just too much for the public to believe. It would have sounded like one last desperate bid to rubbish the German World Cup campaign.

One piece of evidence that could have proved the story had been lying on a stone slab in a German hospital mortuary, but mysteriously Pups's body had been removed and no one knew where it was. In what must have been a major embarrassment for the German authorities, they had lost a dead body. Milton smirked when he heard the news. It made sense now why Stardust was jotting down the name of the hospital. As Jacks had proved in the Gulf War, he did not like to leave a man dead in the field of battle, so they had somehow managed to grab Pups back.

In the days that followed, Milton was commended by his bosses and was promoted. He did not give a damn anymore. His resignation landed on Deputy Assistant Commissioner Dobson's desk along with his detailed report. He was a different person now to the one that had gone undercover in Dubai. The city had changed him; a fact that his wife found out too when he decided that enough was enough and went his separate way.

Chapter 29

Twelve months on and Milton was enjoying a new lease of life. His police career had become a fading memory. He regularly remembered those good times in Dubai, but they always turned sour with the vision of Pups dying on his lap in that Munich street.

He often wondered what had happened to Carson Jacks and the rest of the men. He had come to the conclusion that they had all gone their separate ways. Some probably answered the classifieds in the *Soldier of Fortune* magazine and were fighting in some far-flung foreign land while others, he suspected, had melted back into British society. Jacks would be elsewhere though. He would not return to Britain, but Milton was confident he was probably on some luxury paradise island spending the millions he had made from Expatriatedotcom - or the Germans to be more precise. He would be surrounded by new friends and new women and enjoying an early retirement. Despite everything he had been through in trying to catch his nemesis, he hoped that there was at least some respite for Jacks to rest his troubled mind.

Milton had left the force with the highest of recommendations from his seniors, which landed him his new role, that of head of security with the England football team.

There was no one else more suited to the job. His knowledge of foreign police forces was a bonus and he now spent his time arranging safe passage for the million pound superstars in whom he had previously shown no interest.

He was still single, although his new-found status ensured that there were plenty of opportunities. Maggie had moved on and was seeing another police officer. It had not surprised Milton, who often saw the funny side of his time spent with her and he hoped her new love would live up to the expectations of her father.

Nope - life these days was indeed good for John Milton, who was living life for John Milton, doing things for John Milton and breathing for John Milton. He felt like a free man; reborn and in control of his own destiny.

Depending on which way he looked at it, Carson Jacks was both the worst thing that had ever happened to him and the best. He had lost everything: his wife, career, home; but he felt it was a fair return for what he had now - a new life. He had reinvented himself and had never been happier.

He often thought of Jacks. Like the rest of his disciples, he had come to admire the man, and even more so after he had learned of the experiences he had been through. Jacks may have tricked an army into fighting his one-man crusade against England, but he had also given them a good life at a time when they had little.

In the end, Milton's undercover operation achieved little. Germany, as expected, was awarded the 2006 World Cup and the hooligan ringleaders were still at large, although he knew they would not be showing up at football matches again.

It was just approaching 4.00 p.m. as the England team bus broke through the swathes of fans gathered outside their Swedish hotel. As always, Milton was the first off the bus and he cut a path through the autograph hunters to the rotating doors of the hotel.

He shook hands with the welcoming party and then grabbed the envelopes containing the room keys, which were waiting at reception, and handed them out to the players with whom he was on nickname terms and whose respect he had gained after more than six months on the job. He was their guardian angel and they did what they were told.

He briefed the lads on the basic dos and don'ts before they all retired to their rooms.

Milton had a room to himself and flicked on the TV to catch the tail end of the hourly news bulletin on CNN. This was a habit he was never going to lose when abroad.

But he watched in horror.

The American voice revealed something he had half expected to hear but hoped he would not.

"And we will return to our top story this hour. Six men, believed to be British nationals, have been shot dead by government forces at a diamond mine in Sierra Leone. Details are still coming in, but we are hearing that the six men are believed to have been mercenaries working for a local warlord who had assumed control of the mine earlier this week in a bloody gun battle with government forces. Up to 40 people have been reportedly killed in the firefight, but the six English nationals are believed to be the only foreigners involved."

Milton was glued to the TV for the rest of the evening, but deep down he already knew what was confirmed to him later that evening. The dead were indeed Lenny, JT, Stardust, Chalky, Kirk and finally, as the news reader said:

"Jackie Carson, who was believed to have been killed during the Gulf War but has mysteriously turned up all these years later."

It left Milton motionless. He knew it was coming, but when the words actually confirmed it he did not really know how to react. He was neither sad nor ecstatic. There was nothing to celebrate nor to mourn apart from the fact that it really was now finally over. His life could at last move on ... although, in reality, it had done so already.